THROUGH YOU TO YOU

Stepping Out of Anxiety and Depression
and Into the Next Version of You

MYEISHA THOMPSON

The information given in this book should not be treated
as a substitute for professional medical advice; always
consult a medical practitioner. Any use of information in
this book is at the reader's discretion and risk. Neither the
author nor the publisher can be held responsible for any
loss, claim or damage arising out of the use, or misuse, of
the suggestions made, the failure to take medical advice
or for any material on third-party websites.

ISBN: 979-8-218-41929-5

ISBN: 979-8-218-41930-1 (ebook)

First Edition: April, 2024

For my sonshine—

Thank you for being my reason when I didn't know how to be my own. I'm eternally grateful that God chose me for you.

CONTENTS

Introduction

"What if I'm not really anxious or depressed?"

This was the question I asked myself about eight years ago when—for the millionth time—I found myself completely incapable of getting out of bed on a bright Saturday afternoon.

As a Law & Order: SVU marathon droned on in the background, I found myself oddly curious about the idea of not being depressed or anxious. That curiosity stemmed from a YouTube video I'd listened to the day before, where a physician shared with the interviewer how he'd begun encouraging his diabetic patients to speak differently about their condition.

His advice went something like this: instead of saying "I'm a diabetic", patients should say "I have diabetes" or "I'm working to get my blood sugar under control." The doctor hypothesized that when patients labeled themselves as being something (the "I am" statement), they were making the illness part of their identity. And when a person believes something is a part of who they are, they're less likely to take any meaningful or consistent action to change it.

On the other hand, if patients spoke about the illness as something they possess (the "I have" statement), the disease moved from part of their identity to something they can get rid of or remove. Super interesting, right?

So there I was, lying in bed and staring at the tree-lined horizon from the window of my third-floor apartment, confronted with the idea that I'd suffered from anxiety and depression for so long that the treacherous twins had infiltrated the very bloodstream coursing through my veins, altering the emotional and cognitive oxygen I needed to breathe.

The confrontation was both entirely unexpected and far too heavy for further exploration at that moment. So, like any expert-level self-sabotaging depressed person, I dragged myself to the kitchen, poured an oversized glass of something alcoholic (my guess is vodka or Zinfandel), and crawled back into bed. But the proverbial ball had already begun to roll.

The Only Way Out is Through

Psychological suffering always comes from internal splits between what your uncultured mind believes and what feels deeply true to you.

—Martha Beck

Long before that melancholic day in bed, I'd begun questioning whether anxiety and depression were symptoms rather than illnesses. My childhood, marked by tragedy and trauma, drove me to construct what I thought was a "safe" life. Yet, I later realized that what I'd intended as a refuge was actually a prison—one built on unresolved trauma, allowing me to deny my true self.

Even after 15 years of talk therapy, 15 years of cycling on and off psychiatric medications, 15 years of reading self-help books and attending self-improvement seminars, I still endured devastating financial losses, stalled out in my career, and gained 50 pounds within a seven-month period —all while continuously failing to distract myself with men and martinis. Nothing penetrated my life deep enough to create change or heal the chronic anxiety and depression that, by 2012, left me utterly broke and broken.

It was the unexpected and violent murder of my son's father (my ex-husband) one August afternoon in 2013 that snapped me out of the depressed fog I had lived in for most of my life. His death forced my hand. I had no choice but to somehow free myself from the mental and emotional prison I'd built. I refused to allow my son to finish his childhood with one parent buried and the other one walking around dead. While I was eager to commit to being a better mother, I knew I had to first commit to becoming a better me.

I wish I could say that my path of healing from chronic anxiety and depression was a straight one. It was not. It's been the most grueling, humbling, spirit-opening, expansive experience I've ever encountered. To put it more succinctly: it cracked me wide open.

In her book *The Way of Integrity: Finding the Path to Your True Self*, Harvard-trained sociologist, author and world-renowned life coach Martha Beck argues that trauma and socialization are the two main factors that lead us away from wholeness—mind-body-spirit alignment—and into the depths of prolonged psychological suffering.[1] She uses Dante Alighieri's 14th-century work, *The Divine Comedy*, to illustrate a journey from psychological suffering (like anxiety and depression) to integrity or wholeness. The path is as follows:

- Stage 1: "The dark wood of error." This is a place where we feel lost, exhausted, troubled, and unsure.

- Stage 2: The famous "Dante's Inferno." Here is where we'll find the parts of ourselves that are suffering—the parts trapped in our hell—and set them free using a chisel made of our sense of truth.

- Stage 3: "Purgatory" is the state of cleansing or purification. It's where we shift your external behavior to match our newfound inner truth.

- Stage 4: "Paradise" is where we consistently live our lives in the truth of who we know ourselves to be, operating in full integrity no matter what culture has to say about it.

---

[1] Martha Beck, The Way of Integrity: Finding the Path to Your True Self.

When I read her book in 2021, I fell in love with Beck's metaphor because it was deeply relatable. I recognized my own journey in those stages, finding solace in the fact that this condition of psychological suffering is as old as just about any other human malady.

As someone whose studied yogic philosophy as part of my healing journey, *The Way of Integrity* also reminded me of a famous line from *The Bhagavad Gita*—a 700-verse Hindu scripture—that states, "Yoga is the journey of the self, through the self, to the self."[2]

Here, the term yoga doesn't refer to the Westernized practice ideal that only focuses on the physical aspects or asanas. It refers to the act of yoking, joining or uniting, which is the true definition of yoga. Yoga—like Beck's usage of the term integrity—invites us to work through splintered and disconnected versions of ourselves to a whole undivided version of our minds, bodies, and spirits.

Finally, no book on overcoming chronic anxiety and depression would be complete without addressing the primary source of internal blockages, disconnection, and

---

[2] Maharishi Veda Vyasa, The Bhagavad Gita.

separation from our essential selves—trauma. Given my own experiences marked by both "big T" and "little t" trauma, I understand firsthand the importance of truthfully acknowledging how and where trauma's aftermath manifests in our current experiences.

Often, confronting trauma brings forth guilt, shame, blame and unworthiness. This is when we find ourselves in the inferno. Radical honesty and relentless self-compassion—Stage 2 of the framework—become crucial. We can't extinguish a fire we refuse to acknowledge, nor can we combat it with the same thoughts, feelings, and actions that ignited it. Ultimately, progressing from internal suffering to a consistent expression of your integrated self—Stage 3—requires curiosity, commitment, and self-compassion.

While the stages I outline are largely timeless and universal, how we traverse through them on our journey to healing from chronic anxiety and depression is as unique and individual as we are. More importantly, there are no shortcuts. In fact, any attempt to circumvent the process will hurl you into a vicious and repetitive cycle of failure, shame, guilt and frustration. Sound familiar?

I wrote this book for those who are "sick and tired of being sick and tired" with themselves and their life—even if things seem or look fine on the outside. This book is for anyone willing to admit that how they've been thinking, feeling, and behaving may have gotten them to a perceived place of safety but won't deliver them out of their hell to a place of wholeness or union.

This book and the frameworks I introduce will only be helpful if you're willing to question and examine everything you think you know about anxiety and depression, about who you are, and what loving yourself and your life truly look and feel like.

When I decided to write this book by reverse engineering my own process from the depths of emotional and mental suffering, my first thought—by thought I mean fear—was: "Who am I to write a book about healing?"

And like clockwork, other doubts, fears, and limiting beliefs quickly followed:

- "What makes you think YOU know enough to teach others?"

- "Isn't it hypocritical to proclaim yourself cured when you still have moments of anxiety and low moods?"

But instead of continuing to stand inside the increasingly turbulent stream of fear-based questioning, I stepped outside them. I planted myself on the solid ground of curiosity and self–compassion, allowing me to use the first step in my framework–Identify through self-inquiry. Here's how it went:

Non-judgmental question: What are these thoughts pointing towards inside of me?

"Who am I to write a book about healing?" led me to my real fear: "Will my process, self-reflections, and stories be valuable to anyone?" In other words, "Will it be good enough?

Similarly, the "What makes you think you know enough to teach other people?"question gave way to "Have I studied enough about mental illness, spirituality, psychology, etc. for readers to respect and trust what I've written?"

In other words, "Am I smart enough?"

And lastly, "Isn't it hypocritical to proclaim yourself cured?" led to "Does healing exist outside of societal perfection?" In other words, "Am I enough?"

You may've noticed the recurring theme: enough-ness. More specifically, my fear of writing this book revealed a still ever-present—although far less potent—question of my worthiness. What I also hope you noticed is that my fears weren't the actual problem. Instead, they were acting as my emotional GPS, guiding me to the deeply-rooted location of my real issue.

As such, this book asks readers to set aside the model of chronic anxiety and depression as illnesses and consider the possibility that they're painful symptoms of a deeper wound. While I'm not outright dismissing the validity of the current medical model, I can emphatically state that it proved utterly ineffective as a long-term solution for me.

It wasn't until I committed to traveling through myself with non-judgment, honesty, self-compassion, and an open mind—no matter how long it took or what it looked like—that I was able to free myself from mental suffering. It's my deepest prayer that the process I share will help you do the same.

Before we jump in, I'd like to clarify a few thoughts and give a bit more insight into my approach and intentions.

#1: I refer to the conditions I struggled with as chronic anxiety and depression. This is an important distinction because—as I'll discuss more—anxiety and depression are highly normal emotions to encounter throughout our beautifully complex human experiences. The problem arises when these emotions get stuck. And instead of moving through our physical and mental systems, they morph from feelings to states of being, calcifying as modes of operation. It's that hard, seemingly immovable stuckness we come to know as an illness.

#2: I'm in no way villainizing what I describe as the medical model for treating chronic anxiety and depression. It's not bad or wrong when used for short-term stabilization. In fact, there were a couple of times when psychiatric medications and talk therapy quite literally saved my life! But those were acute incidents. I needed to act quickly, apply pressure to stop the bleeding before I could clean the wound, get stitches, and give it time to heal.

Similarly, long-term treatments with medications coupled with psychotherapy models that have you dredge up the past—without body-based (what professionals refer to as somatic) tools for processing it—don't address the chronic wound.

#3: This is a framework, not a how-to manual. I'm mindful that what got me here may not get you to your desired destination. However, I'm fairly confident that the broad concepts I introduce—along with the various concepts and tools I highlight—will give you what you need to create and walk your own unique path.

#4: Lastly, regarding tools and concepts, I'd like to point out that what I share in these pages is the result of my "throwing spaghetti against the wall and praying that something sticks" approach to healing. I was so tired of feeling broken that I opened myself up to the possibility of just about anything else other than what I'd already tried. Something had to work!

Throughout this book, I'll introduce what I call Ideas to Consider. These are findings from modern neuroscience and psychology research, along with wisdom from ancient traditions and religious teachings. While some of the ideas may not resonate with you or feel applicable to your situation, they've all contributed to my revised understanding of what it means to be free from chronic anxiety and depression.

Stage 1
IDENTIFY

Question Everything

CHAPTER 1

You are the teacher you've been waiting for. You are
the one who can end your own suffering.
—Byron Katie, *Loving What Is*

Good teachers answer questions. Great teachers show you how to answer questions for yourself. But the best teachers encourage you to never stop asking.

Curiosity is an interesting concept. More than a mere point in time where we might have one single question, curiosity—when applied consistently—can describe an ongoing position we take, a guiding principle of sorts for how we move through our day-to-day lives.

Derived from Middle English, the word curious denotes being careful, skillful and eager to learn. Exploring the Latin origins of the term, we find that the root—cura—means care and healing—evoking notions akin to the words accurate or cure.

Curiosity allows us to care and heal without the weight of prior knowledge or biases. A mind and heart posture of curiosity immediately opens us up. It softens us in a way that makes it okay not to have life all buttoned up and figured out. If you allow it, curiosity will wipe the slate clean and shine a light on other possibilities so that you can begin anew.

The Power of Questions When Overcoming Chronic Anxiety and Depression

What happens to our brains when we're asked a question? (see what I did there!)

In short, a question hijacks your thought process. More specifically, questions trigger a mental reflex called instinctive elaboration. That means that once someone poses a question, you literally can't contemplate anything else. Pair this with neuroscience research that concludes the human brain can only think about one idea at a time—sorry to disappoint all you multitaskers—a question remains top of mind until we've somehow answered it, decided that it wasn't worth answering, or actively disengaged in some other way. Amazing, right?

Unfortunately, we can use this power to take over our amazingly complex neurocircuitry as a tool for both healing and harm. As one of my favorite metaphysical and spiritual teachers Michael Beckwith puts it: we have the choice of asking questions that empower or disempower us. That's why a foundational part of overcoming chronic anxiety and depression has been training myself to ask questions that dig deep, require answers via honest self-inquiry, and move me towards feeling integrated, aligned and authentic.

What Does It Mean to Question Everything?

By everything, I don't mean "Why is the sky blue?" or "Why are stop signs red instead of green?" (although the answers to both questions are quite fascinating if you're into useless trivia like some of us!) I use the term everything liberally here for a purpose.

Most of us live our lives based on beliefs, thoughts and feelings that are as unconscious to us as blinking or breathing. They're so deep-seeded and insidious that we've never stopped to question them or to consider if we actually agree with them in real time. I'll give you an example. If you've spent even a few hours in the company of a four or five-year-old child, you've experienced something like the following:

You: Michael, it's time to turn off your iPad and get ready for bed.

Michael: Whhhhhyyyyy?!

You: Because it's important to get a good night's sleep.

Michael: But WHY do I need a good night's sleep?! I want to keep watching my show!

You: You need a good night's sleep so you can be ready for school in the morning.

Michael: Whhhhhyyyyy do I have to go to school anyway?! The only part I like is reading circle!

You: You have to go to school because I said so. Now, let's go get your pajamas...

It may have taken a longer (or shorter) time to get there, but at some point you probably decided to stop trying to reason with the five-year-old. You know what's best and you know you have good intentions, so you asserted your power to make little Michael shutoff his iPad and get ready for bed. This sequence—doing what you're told because it's coming from a trusted (or a feared) authority figure, even though you don't understand—is not too far off from our relationship with our beliefs, thoughts, and feelings.

Much of what we experience as chronic anxiety and depression stems from an internal conflict with the unconscious, unquestioned, and unchecked versions of "because I said so"—the "I" being our families, communities, cultures and society at large. And at some point in our development, that largely unspoken refrain—"because I said so"—morphs into an invisible, omnipresent, all-imposing rule book entitled *Should* . This book details all the things we've been conditioned to believe about how life operates and how we're supposed to move through it.

For instance, you may've questioned if your career, choice of spouse or decision to buy a house instead of traveling the country was right for you. And before you can stop to

19

consider an answer, you unconsciously turn to page 58 in your handy-dandy *Should* manual. There you find that the book's authors demand you aspire to become a doctor or engineer, marry the guy or girl who checks all the right boxes, and settle into your own piece of suburban real estate bliss. None of what you read in the *Should* manual feels quite right, but you do it anyway. This is where we begin laying the groundwork for chronic anxiety, depression or both.

Does this sound familiar? If so, it's because, as Martha Beck explains in *The Way of Integrity*:

> *We learn from our culture how a good person is supposed to behave, and we behave that way. Then we expect the promised rewards: happiness, health, prosperity, true love, solid self-esteem.*

But the equation fails to balance. Even after doing everything we can to be good, we don't feel good. That's why we must first break the spell cast by *Should*.

To do so, we can begin by using questions. Since we're unable to ignore the cognitive magnetism of questions, they're one of the most powerful ways to interrupt the cycle of thoughts, feelings, and actions we experience based on our adherence to *Should*.

Questions force us to pause so we can consciously find and confront underlying assumptions and beliefs. Consistently and nonjudgmentally, questioning our beliefs, our thoughts, and our feelings—pattern interruption—is the first powerful step out of chronic anxiety and depression.

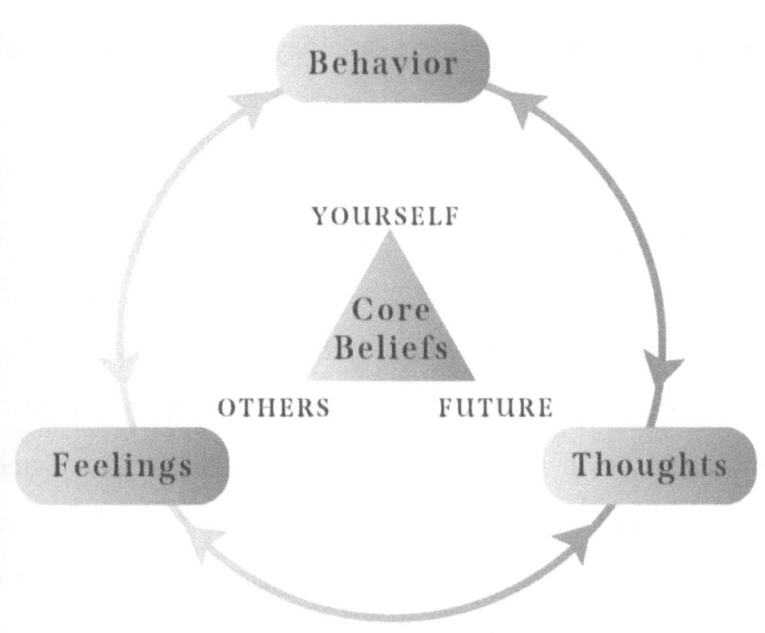

Questioning Your Beliefs

"Hard work pays off." "Better safe than sorry." "Good things come to those who wait." These are ideas that many people in American culture believe and accept as true. But why? Where did these beliefs come from and are they still valid? At this stage of sorting through why you're anxious or depressed, you'll likely find yourself faced with this question: What happens when something you believe deeply (and probably unconsciously) bumps heads with your current knowledge and your lived experience?

In my case—back in my early 20s—a head-on collision with that question ended in my first psychiatric breakdown and a diagnosis of PTSD, anxiety, and depression. At 23 years old, having done everything I believed I was supposed to for success and happiness—earning a college degree, landing a job in marketing, marrying a man I loved and buying a home—I found myself deeply unhappy. Even worse, I had no idea why. I mean, I'd colored inside the lines, followed the script, and ran the plays from society's playbook. So where was my happiness? Where was my contentment? Where was my pride in my accomplishments?

This is the point where most of us make the biggest mistake. Instead of questioning our beliefs about what's *supposed* to make us peaceful, joyful, and whole, we question ourselves. We begin wondering what's wrong with us. We conclude that if we're not happy and excited about our lives, then we're clearly not doing it right. We've somehow not executed the plays as well as we'd thought.

When we decide to question ourselves instead of our beliefs, we've unwittingly laid the foundation for anxiety and depression to build permanent homes in our mental and emotional neighborhoods.

Ideas to Consider: Why We Need Beliefs

In his 2001 best-selling book, *Thinking Fast and Slow*, Nobel Prize winner Daniel Kahneman writes that "For some of our most important beliefs, we have no evidence at all, except that people we love and trust hold these beliefs. Considering how little we know, the confidence we have in our beliefs is preposterous—and it is also essential."

One of the reasons beliefs are essential is that the human brain uses a whopping 20% of the body's energy, even though it only makes up about 2% of an average adult's body mass. Partly an evolutionary survival tool, beliefs allow our brains to maximize energy efficiency, serving as shortcuts for evaluating and making sense of our surroundings in a complex and ever-changing world.

Beliefs arise and develop through direct and indirect teachings from caregivers in childhood, cultural norms, lived experiences, new information, social influence and impactful events.

Ideally, our beliefs evolve continuously as we accumulate new knowledge and experiences in life. However, this usually isn't the case. More often than not, we retain long-held beliefs, even in the face of direct and factual contradiction to their validity. The reason: Humans crave stability.

Just as the more basic parts of the human brain are responsible for stabilizing and balancing critical functions in our body—like breathing, heart rate, blood pressure, body temperature, appetite and hormone levels—our beliefs help maintain a sort of mental stability and consistency in how we interpret and make sense of information about the world around us.

Beliefs provide a form of cognitive homeostasis. This means we're able to maintain a consistent outlook and approach to processing our experiences, rather than having our perspective drastically change every time we get new information. Beliefs operate to preserve a steady and enduring framework of thought that remains relatively undisturbed or disrupted by novel inputs.

Questioning Your Thoughts and Feelings

These pains you feel are messengers. Listen to them.

—*Rumi*

If you've ever been upset with something your child, significant other, or even you yourself have done, you've likely asked— with anger or disgust or despair— "What were you thinking?!" We ask based on our subconscious belief (which both science and spiritually now supports) that our thoughts play a big part in how we act. However, in this scenario, those thoughts aren't the only culprit. A more complete question would be: "What were you feeling and thinking?"

That's because thoughts and feelings exist on a continuum—not a straight path—with behavior. They move so seamlessly into the next that we often mistake one for the other. When a person separates the two, we tend to label them as either cold and antisocial (too much thinking, not enough feeling) or unstable and emotionally erratic (too much feeling, not enough thinking.)

One of the analogies I created for myself to illustrate the tight connection between thoughts and feelings is that of a road trip. I imagine both feelings and thoughts as providing a set of directions.

Let's say thoughts direct us to hop on a five-lane highway with lots of other cars speeding by, changing lanes, and the occasional stop-and-go. While feeling directs us to take the scenic route, a single-lane road lined with trees, winding up and down hills and valleys. But here's the thing: neither is the actual destination!

Actions that align with our beliefs are where we're headed. Thoughts and feelings are just different ways to get there, both of which have their pros and cons. It's here, pulled over on the side of the road, that we get to:

A.   Choose our thoughts exclusively and ignore our feelings.

B.   Ignore our thoughts and act solely based on feelings.

C.   Pause, consider them both, and map a route that takes into consideration the inherent wisdom of each.

When we choose option C, we allow consideration and questioning of our thoughts and feelings to serve as a powerful tool for overcoming chronic anxiety and depression. I've found that training myself to pause, get curious and ask questions induces three important byproducts.

#1: Pattern interruption

Whether you're caught in the grips of a disturbing thought or feeling part of the cycle, the goal is to stop holding on. Stop gripping your thoughts for dear life. Stop holding onto your feelings like they're a cozy, familiar blanket. Stop it all.

Think of the pattern interruption as the part of the road trip where you realize you're lost and the best course of action is to pull over and look at what Google Maps has to say.

#2: Creating space

Viktor Frankl, psychiatrist, Holocaust survivor and author of the book *Man's Search for Meaning*, famously concluded:

Between stimulus and response there is a space. In that space is our power to choose our response. In our response lies our growth and our freedom.

Unfortunately, so many of us miss the part about having a choice in how we respond to life because we don't make the space. Thankfully, stopping and asking questions automatically creates room for redirection, an alternate route that encompasses more than we may have previously considered.

#3: Grounding in reality

This isn't the place where I want to dive into the nature of reality. But I'm hoping that we can agree on reality existing in the present moment—not the past or the future. What's real or true is what's right now.

Just like in my road trip analogy, we can only plot a path to our destination based on the current location. Instead of trying to reroute based on where you were three miles (or months) ago, or where you'll be once you figure out how to get moving again, questioning your thoughts and feelings stops you. It demands that you look at what's real in the moment to move forward in earnest.

So the next time you find yourself stuck in an episode of high anxiety or deep depression, remember: stop, then ask yourself what you're thinking *and* feeling. From there, you'll be better positioned to decide how you can move forward, understanding that you need both to get you out of anxiety or depression and into aligned action.

Ideas to Consider: Challenging the Belief about Mental Disorders as Chemical Imbalances

"Will six sessions of CBT, designed to target 'unhelpful' thinking styles, really be effective for someone who doesn't know how they're going to feed their family for another week? Antidepressants aren't going to eradicate the relentless racial trauma a black man is surviving in a hostile workplace.. Unsurprisingly, mindfulness isn't helping children who are navigating poverty, peer pressure and competitive exam-driven school conditions, where bullying and social media harm are rife. I'm a psychologist – and I believe we've been told devastating lies about mental health." **Dr. Sanah Ahsan**

The work of British psychiatrist, researcher, and professor Dr. Joanna Moncrieff challenges what she calls the disease-centered model for understanding mental disorders.

She contends that, by comparing the treatment for chronic depression to that of insulin for diabetes, both the profession of psychiatry at large and the pharmaceutical

---

industry have elevated and continue to champion a scientifically unsupported claim: chronic depression is caused by a chemical imbalance. She further challenges the claim that psychoactive prescription drugs successfully treat mental disorders by targeting a chemical imbalance in the brain.

Published in 2014 by Dr. Moncrieff and colleagues,

"The serotonin theory of depression: A systematic umbrella review of the evidence" skillfully challenges the widely-accepted cause-and-effect relationship between low serotonin levels and the prevalence of chronic depression. Speaking of the ground-breaking meta-analysis of, Dr. Moncrieff provides the following summary:

"We conducted a systematic umbrella review of the main areas of research on links between serotonin and depression, including research on serotonin levels, the main serotonin metabolite, serotonin receptors, the serotonin transporter, serotonin depletion studies and genetic studies. None of this research convincingly supported the theory that depression is caused by low serotonin. In contrast, studies showed that experiencing adverse life events strongly predicted someone's chances of becoming depressed later in life. The findings should prompt a re evaluation of the nature and value of antidepressants."

Dr. Moncrieff says that this approach only "medicalize misery" by attempting to neatly classify the vast and complex nature of negative human experiences that are likely the root cause of mental illness (like childhood trauma grief, economic distress or insecurity). Her work champions the idea of treating mental illnesses like anxiety and depression as human suffering that has roots in distressing personal, social, moral, and political environments.

"I do not think the majority of the situations that psychiatrists help to manage are diseases or illnesses, or things that arise from the physical body. I think they are better understood as forms of behavior that are unusual sometimes irrational and unpredictable, and socially problematic for one reason or another. I am not convinced therefore that it is logical for them to be regarded as part of the terrain of medicine."

Books by Dr. Joanna Moncrieff

The Myth of the Chemical Cure: a critique of psychiatric drug treatment, Palgrave, 2008.

A Straight Talking Introduction to Psychiatric Drugs, PCCS Books, 2009.

The Bitterest Pills: the troubling story of antipsychotic drugs, Palgrave, 2013.

Practice Being the Unbiased Witness

CHAPTER

You can look deep within yourself, to the core of your being, and decide that you don't want the weakest part of you running your life.
—Michael A. Singer, The Untethered Soul

So you've mustered up the courage to ask yourself some of the tough questions about what you believe, think, feel, and why you act the way you do. Now what? Chances are, the simple, honest, unambiguous answers you'd hope would immediately pop into your mind didn't.

Instead, after asking yourself "Why do I fill my refrigerator and cupboards with unhealthy foods when I'm supposed to be following a weight loss program?" or "Why am I still working here after 11 years when I hated it after the first 18 months?" you probably did one of the following:

#1: You shut down. Like a wave during high tide, the sheer number of negative, emotionally charged answers rushed into your mind, engulfed you, and dragged you under. Fully overwhelmed, you decided not to take note of any of them. As a bonus, you probably engaged in your go-to distraction (aka coping mechanism) like scrolling on social media, grabbing the bag of chocolate chip cookies from the pantry, or opening the app for your favorite online store to see what's on sale. These actions help you ride out the wave of emotions until you're able to comfortably resume mental autopilot.

#2: You got defensive. Your internal dialogue began rattling off the myriad reasons why you can't just do what you want to do. I mean, you have adult responsibilities, after all! The mortgage won't pay itself while you find a new job. The kids won't stop requiring food, shelter, and clothing while you "find yourself." It's silly—no, downright childish of you—to think you can make such a big change and leave a perfectly good, well-paying job just because you're unhappy.

In either case you never really answered the question. Like a reflex, you either closed off the mental space the question created, or you immediately filled that space with judgments, anger, and excuses. Neither will help you free yourself from the cage that chronic anxiety and depression has locked you in.

Me? I was captain of team Shut Down. In 2012, when I began taking inventory of my physical health (I'd gained 50 pounds in just over a year,) my finances (filed for bankruptcy in 2010,) my parenting (still struggling to connect emotionally with my son,) my stalled career (I hated just about every job or freelance project I took,) my raggedy-ass romantic relationships (just... yuk,) my mind hit the emergency break. What could've possibly happened inside of me in six years that I'd gone from a physically fit, financially sound, career-driven, married woman with a beautiful home and children to... *this*?!

How could I possibly deal with the flood of guilt and confusion and shame that threatened to drown me as soon as I tried to sit in the space between stimulus (the questions) and my response? Short answer: I didn't deal with it at all. As any high-performing member of team Shut

Down would do, I continued distracting myself with food and sleep and alcohol and sex for another year or so.

But my questioning—my sincere and desperate inquiry about what was happening inside of me—was like a flare gun from my subconscious. Its bright light pierced the darkness, signaling that although I was still locked in a cage of self-destructive patterns that reinforced anxiety and depression, I was alive in there. And where there's life, there's also hope.

This is a good place to pause and remind you of my central claims about why so many of us struggle to break free from chronic anxiety and depression—even after years of treatment. Through my lived experiences, other firsthand accounts, and extensive research, I've concluded that:

- The Westernized medical model fails because it focuses on treating symptoms instead of identifying root causes and providing sustainable solutions.

- While effective in acute occurrences or breakdowns, treating chronic anxiety and depression with prescription medication and talk therapy falls short for most chronic cases.

- Ignoring the mind–body–spirit connection when treating these disorders creates a false binary between mental and physical health, making it harder to connect to our spiritual selves or identify and process all of the trauma we hold in our bodies.

If you're fed up with the medical treatment roller coaster and have decided to guide yourself out of the internal maze of funhouse mirrors, things can get a little scary at this point. You take the important first step of questioning and self-inquiry, only to find yourself shutting down or getting defensive. Don't panic. This is where you meet the unbiased witness.

The unbiased witness, explained

If you've ever watched a few episodes of any television courtroom series, then you know the importance of witness testimony. In particular, the most effective and valuable witnesses are those with unimpeachable character and no ulterior motives, the ones who can recount their observations without the filter of their own emotional involvement or judgment.

These are the witnesses that both prosecution and defense attorneys clamor for—the ones who jurors trust. These are the people who, when taking the stand, have nothing to gain by imposing their own views on what they've seen or heard. They're simply delivering the facts as they understand them, leaving the courtroom, and returning to business as usual.

Now, let's imagine your internal mental and emotional drama as an episode of a courtroom drama. But instead of different actors, you get to play all of the characters. In this special extended episode, you're the plaintiff who pressed the charges and the defendant who thinks she's innocent. You're the prosecutor who's determined to make you pay for your wrongdoing and the defense attorney who presents every argument for why your actions were justified. You're the judge and the jury. But most importantly: you get to play the role of the witness.

In his book, *The Untethered Soul,* author Michael Singer describes becoming the witness of your internal drama as the most important part of true emotional and spiritual growth. He explains that:

You are not the voice of the mind—you are the one who hears it. If you don't understand this, you will try to figure out which of the many things the voice says is really you... People want to discover which of these voices, which of these aspects of their personality, is who they really are. The answer is simple: none of them.

So, who are you, then? If you're not the one talking to yourself on the inside, who (or what) is in there? It's easy to go down the rabbit hole and get lost in the details here. Don't. This is a valid question that we'll get into later. But for now, this is where you'll need to take my and Michael Singer's word for it. You are the energy—or consciousness—listening and watching. You are the one witnessing it all.

Those thoughts, words, and emotions: not you. All the doom, gloom, despair and ruminating and panicking: not you. Although this may not make sense yet, I hope—at least on some level—you feel some relief! That tribe of maniacs who don't agree about much (ever!) and seemingly rule every waking moment of your life—they're not the core of what makes you, you. In fact, the more you're able to disconnect those thoughts and actions from who you truly are and instead begin observing them like the rowdy band of misfits they are, the sooner you'll experience a sense of ease internally.

The unbiased witness in action

So why is embracing your role as the witness so important to moving past anxiety and depression? Let's revisit the courtroom analogy for a bit. In television and in real life, we've all seen how reliable eyewitness testimony can make or break the outcome of a trial. And before DNA evidence, the unbiased, first-hand recounting of events often constituted the only sure thing to base a ruling or verdict on.

This is what happens when you practice becoming the witness in your own life. You're not swayed by good or bad, right or wrong, what was supposed to happen versus what actually happened. You—like the most impactful witnesses—only concern yourself with the facts of your situation.

For example, let's say you let your ex wiggle his or her way back into your life for the third (or 13th) time. And, just like the sun rises in the east and sets in the west, it only takes a few weeks before the whole situation spirals right back into the depths of hell you pulled it from.

That first night alone after you decided it was over goes as it always has—shitty. You pour a glass of wine, walk into your bedroom, plop down on the side of your bed, and turn on a cooking competition or a Netflix original series you've been meaning to check out. As soon as you settle in to watch, here comes that voice: your messy mental roommate. It cozies up right next to you and starts the conversation about how she knew it wouldn't work, how stupid you are, and how she tried to talk you out of it but you wouldn't listen.

At this point in the program, she gets louder and begins shouting about how much of an absolute asshole your ex is, and that his inability to think of anyone but themselves makes them a horrible person and partner.

As you continue tuning in and agreeing with your messy mental roommate, the pit of your stomach begins twisting and turning. Your breath gets shallow. Your heart may even begin to race a bit. That double pour of wine is almost gone and you're beginning to participate in the conversation. But what if you didn't join in?

What if, instead of agreeing with and adding to the list of judgements and opinions, you became the witness. You pay attention to the fact that your stomach feels funny and your breath isn't moving past your chest. You take note— but no judgments! Instead, you nod your head, maybe even thank your messy mental roommate for sharing her thoughts and feelings, then file those bits of information away to report back to the authorities. As the witness, you're free to turn your focus to taking slow, deep inhales and exhales that reduce your heart rate and untie the knots in your stomach. You remain observant and unbiased as the inner critic runs out of steam and lets you rest—at least for the time being.

If you were able to read that and follow the story, then you can do this! Just like I trained myself to do, you begin by narrating your mental dramas. You make a conscious decision to read the subtitles instead of acting out the script. Spiritual teachings refer to this as cultivating witness consciousness which, as Michael Singer writes, serves as a linchpin skill in the process of healing. As the witness, you're willing to ask yourself all of the important questions about what's beneath the anxiety and depression, then sit in the darkness and cold of honest answers. No more shutting down. No more defensiveness. You're identifying the root causes and are well on your way to freeing yourself.

Recognize that unlearning is the highest form of learning.

—*Rumi*

Practice makes progress

I cannot stress enough how important it is to show yourself God-like grace during this part of Stage 1. Put on your helmet and knee pads because I guarantee you're going to bust your butt and take more than a few nasty falls while learning to ride the bike of being the unbiased witness. Good news: once you get the hang of it, another (brighter and less panicked) world of possibilities for moving through your life opens. Not-so-good news: the deeper the questions and the more painful the answers, the less likely you'll be able to avoid slipping into old patterns of shutdown or defensiveness.

What I've learned from the millions of times I've fallen back into participating with the voice in my head (and sometimes the friends she invites over!) is that it's not whether I visit, but how long I stay. As the witness, you're still burdened with the weights and temptations of acting out decades of internal drama. The difference now is that you've experienced the other side. Visiting the old neighborhood will lose its appeal and familiarity, and getting back out quickly will become your reflex.

I'm nowhere near the point of staying in the seat of the witness 24/7, but I'm there far more times than not. How do I know? Life has given me plenty of opportunities to prove it over the past five years! From sending my only son to college, relocating to a new state, to quitting my job to work for myself and while going back to school for a completely new career, from thinking I was ready to find love only to decide I'm having way too much fun loving on myself—amidst the pivoting, turning, doubting and learning—the witness feels more like home. It's my set point, even when I spend time away. It's from this new home that we can begin the next block of work in the journey to ourselves.

Ideas to Consider: Your Brain and Your Mind Are Not the Same Thing

"...in recent years we've learned that the human brain is actually a master of deception, and your experiences and actions do not reveal its inner workings. Your mind is in fact an ongoing construction of your brain, your body, and the surrounding world." Lisa Feldman Barrett

Both ancient spiritual traditions and modern neuroscience agree: while the brain and the mind are unique and separate neither can operate fully without the other.

A common analogy used to describe the differences and interconnections between the brain and the mind is that of computer hardware and software. The brain is the physical organ–the hardware–made up of structures and components that send electrical signals and information. The mind is the software that runs it.

Neuroscientist Carolyn Leaf, Ph.D. teaches that "the mind is energy, and it generates energy through thinking, feeling and choosing." Our thoughts, feelings, and actions, in turn alter the physical connections in our brain. This phenomenon known as neuroplasticity, gives us the uniquely human capacity to change and update how we perceive and interact with the world around us and within us.

Brain	Mind
a tangible organ of the body	an intangible energy that is characterized as having both conscious and unconscious states
Controls physiology (how our bodies work) as half of the central nervous system (the spinal cord is the other half)	Controls what we think and how we feel; shapes beliefs, emotions, and memory
Can develop diseases and physical traumas that are measurable through diagnostic technologies like x-ray, MRI, or blood tests	Can not be found in a physical part of the body; abnormilites or disturbances characterized as disorders, not diseases

Books by Lisa Feldman Barrett

Seven and a Half Lessons About the Brain, Houghton Mifflin Harcourt, 2020

How Emotions Are Made: The Secret Life of the Brain, Houghton Mifflin Harcourt, 2017

Stage 2
EMBRACE

Meet Yourself Where You Are: The Role of Trauma in Chronic Anxiety and Depression

CHAPTER

We are all traumatized by life, by its unpredictability, its randomness, its lack of regard for our feelings and the losses it brings.
—Mark Epstein, MD, *The Trauma of Everyday Life*

"I need to go."

Those were the words I found myself saying to my husband as we stood at the kitchen counter of our home, less than a month after we'd returned from our first family vacation in Jamaica. The day before, I'd walked into my boss's office—the VP of marketing at a growing tech start-up—and told him that I needed to quit. Both my husband and my boss were shocked and concerned. Both men— each more than a decade older than me—knew something I did not: I was smack-dab in the middle of losing my shit! I was in the middle of a full-on "I can't do this anymore," "Whatever happens, happens" mental breakdown.

As grace would have it, neither my husband nor my boss fought me. Instead, my boss convinced me to take some time off to rest and regroup. My husband and his friend loaded a few of my things into the back of our pickup truck and moved me into a small one-bedroom apartment on a quiet tree-lined street about 10 minutes from our home. My husband also told me that I needed to get professional psychiatric help—immediately.

Trauma: the most important variable in the healing equation

Trauma is an indivisible part of human existence. It takes many forms but spares no one.

—Mark Epstein, MD, *The Trauma of Everyday Life*

My breakdown, although seemingly sudden and swift in its fallout, had been a slow, surreal train that departed the station in early childhood and was fueled by instability and tragedy along its route. My brilliant knack for deep emotional suppression and unconscious numbing helped the locomotive build up steam until this unceremonious derailment when I was 23 years old.

My first response: Run! Get the hell out of it ("it" being my life) immediately!

My second response: Freeze. Specifically, sitting in a little wicker café chair from Pier 1 Imports, tucked in the corner next to the floor-to-ceiling window in the brownstone apartment I'd rented, experiencing a wave of emotions that felt like everything and nothing all at once.

As I'd learn during my first few therapy sessions, those uncontrollable urges to run and then shelter in place were three of the classic trauma responses: fight, flight, and freeze.

Before therapy, the idea that I'd somehow been traumatized hadn't occurred to me. On the contrary, the lenses through which I viewed my life were ones of awe and gratitude. I mean, how did I somehow navigate my way through growing up with drug-addicted parents, the sudden loss of my maternal grandmother and primary caregiver while I was in sixth grade, make it to a prestigious university on an academic scholarship, have my mother die in my arms of a sudden heart attack during winter break of my freshman year—then bury my only sister, get married, bury my father who died from complications of a healing gunshot wound, graduate undergrad with honors, land a great job in (then) emerging field of tech marketing—all by the age of 21?

What did any of that have to do with where I'd found myself: sitting frozen in front of my window, staring at the park across the street for what felt like days on end? Turns out, it had everything to do with it.

Quick moment of transparency: this is the chapter that scared me the most to write. That's because a topic as complex, as pervasive, as individual as trauma warrants far more than a quick glance or cursory examination— especially as it relates to chronic anxiety and depression.

For perspective, a simple search on Amazon for paperback books with PTSD (post-traumatic stress disorder) in the title returned thousands of results. The list included everything from coloring books to workbooks to guides and how-to manuals for healing your inner wounded child. The sheer number of books on the topic, coupled with the casual tossing around of the term in popular culture and on social media, made it clear to me that connecting the dots without getting too technical would require a fair amount of focus and intention. The approach I landed on: start with the basics.

Understanding trauma

So, what is trauma, anyway? Well, it depends on who you ask.

For starters, the term itself comes from the Greek language and translates as "wound." If we move forward a few centuries to a more modern, clinical definition, the Diagnostic and Statistical Manual of Mental Disorders, 5th Edition (DSM-5), defines trauma as when an individual person is exposed to actual or threatened death, serious injury, or sexual violence. [3]

When considering its link to chronic anxiety and depression, one of the most functional and helpful definitions of trauma I've come across is from Dr. Gabor Maté, a world-renowned addiction and childhood development expert. In his work, Dr. Maté has found that "Trauma is not what happens to you. Trauma is what happens inside of you in response to what happens to you."

In our understanding of trauma, if we conflate what happened (or didn't happen in cases of neglect) with the harm it caused, we run the risk of never quite getting to the heart of the matter. The trauma isn't the bomb itself: it's the rubble and debris and carnage. It is the aftermath.

This is one reason why people can experience the same car accident, grow up in the same under-resourced neighborhood, or live in the same abusive household, and be left with

---

3 Center for Substance Abuse Treatment (US). (1970, January 1). A review of the literature. Trauma-Informed Care in Behavioral Health Services. https://www.ncbi.nlm.nih.gov/books/NBK207192/

vastly different outcomes. If trauma is about what happens inside of us—and we're all individual and unique on the inside—then it's no surprise that the duration and severity of mental, emotional, and physical problems that ensue varies from person to person.

However, there are enough documented similarities for us to find patterns that allow better understanding and healing. Starting from Dr. Maté's clear, simple definition of trauma, we can better understand the link between it and chronic anxiety and depression.

Ideas to Consider: Adverse Childhood Experiences Live Well Into Our Adulthoods

In the mid-1990's, Kaiser Permanente teamed up with the Centers for Disease Control to conduct the ACE (Adverse Childhood Experiences) Study with a group of 17,00 participants insured through Kaiser Permanente. The goal: find out how traumatic childhood events occurring before a person's 18th birthday may negatively affect adult health.

Study data revealed a direct link between childhood trauma and adult onset of chronic disease, incarceration, and employment challenges. Incidents of various chronic illnesses and social challenges increased as the number of ACEs increased.

The 10 ACEs were defined as having experienced the following before the 18th birthday:	
Emotional abuse	Mental illness of a family member
Physical abuse	Parents divorced/separated
Sexual abuse	Family member incarcerated
Mother treated violently	Emotional neglect
Substance abuse in the home	Physical neglect

Subsequent studies have found that adults who experience a high number of ACEs—4 or more out of 10—have higher incidence of anxiety, depression, obesity, substance abuse, attempted suicide, and an overall life expectancy that 20 years less than adults who don't have any ACEs.

Dealing with trauma: the turning point in moving past anxiety and depression

My first psychiatrist was a godsend. Having treated hundreds of veterans with PTSD early in her training—then other trauma survivors in her private practice—Dr. Murphy was all too familiar with variations on my story. After our initial session where I answered questions about my childhood and just about everything leading up to my current breakdown, she provided a diagnosis: PTSD, major depression, and anxiety. She sent me home with a prescription for an antidepressant, an anti-anxiety medication, and a recommendation to see her once a week so that we could get me back into my life.

I don't remember much about how I felt other than a sense of relief. There were actual names and diagnoses and medical billing codes for the internal hell I'd found myself in. I wasn't miserable for no reason. Even better: there were pills I could take! The idea that I could treat a chemical imbalance in my brain so that I would no longer want to escape from my body and from my life seemed too good to be true. Turns out, it was.

The panacea I thought I'd found in medications and talk therapy was short-lived. Yes, I was able to drag myself out of bed more often and not experience horrific panic attacks multiple times a week. However, I still felt disconnected, empty, and disinterested in much of what was supposed to be a normal, happy life. At this point, frustration and confusion kicked in because if this way of fixing myself didn't work , what would?

I expressed my concerns and frustrations to my physiatrist, She encouraged me to not lose hope in the process. Even though Dr. Murphy leaned heavily on pharmaceutical interventions and cognitive behavioral therapy (CBT), she also introduced me to Eastern medicine practices that incorporated energy healing and using somatic (body-based) techniques to release the trauma from my body's memory. We began acupuncture and moxibustion treatments at the beginning of each weekly session. We'd sit on the floor to help me ground myself as we talked through my deep wounds from not having my mother because of her heroin addiction, to my maternal grandmother (who was my primary caregiver) suddenly passing away when I was 12 years old. She'd have me place one hand on my stomach and the other on my heart as I recounted having my mother die suddenly in my arms a few weeks before my 19th birthday, or described the various instances of childhood sexual abuse I faced.

What I didn't fully understand at the time (I don't remember if she ever explained it to me) was that Dr. Murphy was slowly guiding me into my bodily experiences and sensations as an active part of my trauma recovery. All of the talking and rehashing and figuring out and "aha" moments would be for naught if I didn't get out of my head and into my body. I had to step back into my physical body and somehow feel and release the emotions I'd repressed for more than a decade.

The numbness that had served as my shock absorber and allowed me to move through multiple traumas (seemingly unphased) into a productive young adulthood had morphed into a huge roadblock called anxiety and depression. The only way through was to feel the full spectrum of my emotions and—finally—let them move through me.

Ideas to Consider: The Connection between Feelings and Emotions

A significant part of what we experience as negative emotions involves what our bodies feel via uncomfortable involuntary reactions from our muscles, as well as our respiratory, pulmonary, and digestive systems. Our emotions and bodily sensations are so interconnected that we often consider our "feelings" and "emotions" one in the same.

That's why a powerful tool for moving past chronic anxiety and depression is understanding what bodily sensations occur when you experience particular negative emotions. From there, you're better equipped to process and release those feelings and return to a state of calm and well being. We can identify sensations using what scientists call interoception.

Interoception is the process of sensing signals from the body, like how fast the heart is beating, whether your breathing is deep or shallow, or if you need to use the toilet.

"Researchers and clinicians are recognising interoception as a key mechanism to mental and physical health, where understanding our body's signals helps us understand and regulate emotional and physical states," says Dr. Helen Weng at the University of California San Francisco.

The results of a 2014 study, conducted by computational and statistics expert Enrico Glerean and colleagues, mapped 13 emotions to specific body parts by noting what body parts activated or had decreased activation when participants were experiencing particular emotions. The findings were consistent across participants in different West European and East Asian cultures, supporting the biological (opposed to sociological) basis of the body sensation patterns.

Below is a chart of where people typically experience bodily sensations related to common negative emotions.

Emotion	Increased activation in:	Decreased activation in:
Fear	upper half of the body, excluding the arms; also some activation in the feet	
Sadness	chest and head	arms, legs, and feet
Anxiety	areas above the pelvis, excluding the arms	arms, legs, and feet
Depression		lower body
Shame	torso and head	arms, legs, and feet
Envy	chest and head	legs
Contempt	head and hands	pelvic and leg area

Phases of trauma healing

For me, releasing trauma hasn't been a short or linear process. I had no clue of the depth and severity of my numbness and emotional disassociation until I started digging. What took me over 20 years to experience took just about as long to move past. There've been false starts, setbacks, and moments of disappointment and despair—within the healing process and with myself.

At some point in my 30s, as I approached releasing trauma for what felt like the thousandth time, a pivotal question shook me out of the cycle of "never getting it right" thinking. I asked myself: Why should I expect a trip that took a certain amount of time one way to be so much shorter on the way back? Even with a faster, more efficient mode of transportation, the distance is the same.

I'd traveled so far away from integrity and wholeness that it couldn't have possibly taken as short a time as I'd unconsciously believed. Somehow, I'd come to expect that all of the knowledge I'd gained on anxiety, depression, and PTSD would quickly catapult me to a better place. It did not.

Information isn't power. It's potential. The willingness to show up again and again and stumble through the application of that knowledge—as messy and imperfect as that process will likely be—is the true source of your healing power. That was my experience. By letting go of a "get healed quick" mindset and replacing it with "get healed or die trying", I opened myself to the beauty of the process instead of the promise of a particular outcome. Looking back on what that entailed, here are the two phases I cycled through as part of my trauma-healing journey.

So self-acceptance does not mean self-admiration or even self-liking at every moment of our lives, but tolerance for all our emotions, including those that make us feel uncomfortable.

—Gabor Maté, Scattered Minds: The Origins and Healing of Attention Deficit Disorder

Phase 1: Meet yourself where you are

I'm no Bible scholar. In truth, I'm not even a Christian in the most basic sense (accepting Jesus as my savior.) However, I love and have studied the teachings of Jesus, each time walking away with some of the most profound and practical advice for being a better human. One of the most impactful Bible stories I studied is in the fifth chapter of the book of John, often referred to as "the healing at the pool."

There in Jerusalem, we find Jesus in conversation with a man near a pool. The pool area, which was surrounded by five covered colonnades, served as a regular meeting place for "the blind, the lame, the paralyzed" to lie and wait for an angel to stir (or trouble) the waters, imbuing it with healing powers. The story goes that whoever was first to enter the water after the angel stirred it would be healed. But it's in verse five where things get interesting:

5] And a certain man was there, which had an infirmity thirty and eight years.

[6] When Jesus saw him lie, and knew that he had been now a long time in that case, he saith unto him, Wilt thou be made whole?

[7] The impotent man answered him, Sir, I have no man, when the water is troubled, to put me into the pool: but while I am coming, another steppeth down before me.

[8] Jesus saith unto him, Rise, take up thy bed, and walk.

[9] And immediately the man was made whole, and took up his bed, and walked: and on the same day was the sabbath.

(King James version)

So, what do these Bible verses have to do with meeting yourself where you are? Plenty!

In the most literal sense, it shows us that even the most powerful healer in the Christian faith made a point to visit the exact location of the sick people—not the other way around. But a less obvious correlation—and the part that immediately gave me pause when I first read it—was the question he asked: "Wilt thou be made whole?"

Just like Jesus asked the man at the pool, the first question we must ask ourselves is this: Am I willing to heal? It may seem like a no-brainer, but many of us are like the man Jesus healed in more ways than one. Not only have we been unconsciously stuck in old patterns of thinking and believing what and how healing can occur but we're also waiting for someone and something outside of ourselves to take us there. Spoiler alert: it ain't happenin'!

What's often overlooked when considering the glow and warmth cast by the prospect of healing is the source: the burning fire of change. That's right! At its core, healing is a deep, uncomfortable—sometimes even painful—seismic change in how you process your inner and outer worlds. It shifts everything. It troubles the waters. It carves out new emotional and mental streams for feelings, thoughts, and actions to synchronously flow together. But first, you must be willing.

To meet yourself where you are means to bridge the gap between your expectations and what's happening right now—in real time. Have you been willing to heal, or have fear, guilt, shame, frustration, anger, or even numbness kept you from acknowledging your location on the path? If so, you're certainly not alone.

When meeting yourself where you are, you must suspend judgment. Instead of ruminating on how things should be or how you should feel and behave, you must create space for acknowledging and accepting the here and now of your suffering. See it. Feel it. Make peace with its existence. Only from a place of complete willingness to change—from the deepest parts of yourself—can you take up your bed and start walking in the direction of peace and wholeness.

Likewise, trauma is a psychic injury, lodged in our nervous system, mind, and body, lasting long past the originating incident(s), triggerable at any moment. It is a constellation of hardships, composed of the wound itself and the residual burdens that our woundedness imposes on our bodies and souls: the unresolved emotions they visit upon us; the coping dynamics they dictate; the tragic or melodramatic or neurotic scripts we unwittingly but inexorably live out; and, not least, the toll these take on our bodies.

—**Gabor Mate´**, *The Myth of Normal*

Phase 2: Acknowledge and process the pain

The sudden death of my son's father (my ex-husband) in 2013 shocked me into the willingness and humility needed to finish digging myself out of my own decades-long mental and emotional turmoil so that I could be fully present for my son. As life would have it, I'd found myself in the aftermath of yet another trauma storm— but this time, it was different.

Without my conscious awareness, my body refused to cooperate with the go numb and keep it moving routine I attempted to replicate from my childhood and early adulthood. This time around, my body and mind conspired to send me exactly what they knew would stop me in my tracks and get my undivided attention—chronic physical pain.

I was diagnosed with fibromyalgia and an autoimmune condition in early 2018. Less than a year before, I'd undergone a surgery on my lumbar spine to cure debilitating sciatica and other lower back pain. All of this seemingly came out of the blue, as my only other physical illnesses throughout my life were recurring sinus infections. I hadn't even had a cavity as an adult.

Yet there I was, in my early 40s, grappling with the idea of managing chronic painful physical conditions for the rest of my life. I refused to accept it. At this time, while I still struggled with bouts of severe anxiety and depression, they were much fewer and far between, and I was no longer on psychiatric medications.

From the back pain that made walking a chore to the full-body onslaught of a fibromyalgia flare up, and an immune system that was attacking itself, my body sounded an alarm so consistent and painful that I had no choice but to acknowledge and heed the blaring physiological alarms. Fortunately, I stumbled upon an acupuncturist who introduced me to the practice of letting physical pain be my emotional and spiritual guide.

During my first session with the acupuncturist, she started by asking about my life and what I'd been going through in the months leading up to my chronic pain conditions. Something immediately clicked in my heart and mind! I knew that what she began explaining about the connections between chronic physical pain and people's response to emotional pain and trauma was indeed one of the root causes of my current experience.

In fact, answering her questions helped me realize that the physical pain could be a gift if I took the time to unwrap it. Caring for my body turned into a self-discovery mission—inside and out. What thoughts and feelings preceded a fibromyalgia flare? How much sleep and exercise did I get on days that I felt less anxious? Why does a round of deep breathing or five minutes of meditation soothe my low back pain? Once I stopped fighting the physical pain and got curious about what trapped experiences and emotions it may represent, I not only saw physical improvements but I unlocked a powerful new vehicle for moving past chronic anxiety and depression.

What was once considered "woo-woo" in Western medicine and culture has now been born out as scientific fact: our bodies record emotional experience. Unfortunately, modern American health practices have largely disregarded the body's connection to mental health outside of the chemicals created by our brains (like serotonin and dopamine.) The result: Many of us ignore the physical imbalances that are part of how we experience trauma. Left unchecked, our bodies continue to communicate signals of pain and dis-ease to our minds, which reinforce the cycle of negative thoughts and emotions.

This is an excellent place to pause and clarify another often used but rarely defined term: emotions. Merriam-Webster defines emotions as "conscious mental reactions (such as anger or fear) subjectively experienced as strong feelings usually directed toward a specific object and typically accompanied by physiological and behavioral changes in the body."

Simply put: emotions involve both the mind (mental reactions) and the body (physiological changes).

Just think about some of the common phrases we use to describe how we experience emotions. "My husband is a pain in the neck." " The way my coworker complains all day makes me sick." "My stomach sank when I got the disappointing news from my boss." It's not a coincidence that we use bodily sensations to describe our emotional states. They're inextricably linked.

Brain scans have shown that the same areas activate when we're in both physical and emotional pain.[4] Also, our immune system's ability to fight off even a common cold becomes compromised during protracted periods of mental and emotional stress. The communication network that connects our bodies and minds—ultimately dictating how we experience much of our lives—is called The autonomic nervous system (ANS.)

Without getting too technical (I hope), here are five things you need to know about the ANS as it relates to trauma, anxiety, and depression.

#1: There are two parts of the ANS: The sympathetic nervous system and the parasympathetic nervous system.

#2: The sympathetic nervous system governs our flight, flight, and freeze responses to real or imagined threats. The

---

4 Sussex Publishers. (n.d.). Emotional and physical pain activate similar brain regions. Psychology Today. https://www.psychologytoday.com/us/blog/body-sense/201204/emotional-and-physical-pain-activate-similar-brain-regions

parasympathetic nervous system is responsible for the rest and digest functions in our bodies, allowing cells and organs to recover and bring our bodies back into a calm state.

#3: Both parts of the ANS impact our heart rate, blood pressure, and breathing by signaling specific chemical releases. The sympathetic nervous system speeds up those bodily functions (i.e. racing heart, increased blood pressure, fast and shallow breathing) while the parasympathetic nervous system slows them down.

#4: Research findings suggest that negative emotions can activate the sympathetic response and positive emotions can turn on the parasympathetic response.

#5: Fluid, regulated movement between the two branches of the ANS results in connection and integration between our bodies and minds that promote physical and mental health.

People who have experienced trauma in their lives have a higher baseline of physiological arousal. This makes them more sensitive to stress and more likely to activate their fight, flight or freeze response system. Traumatic experiences are stored in the body as physical sensations and emotions, not memories.

—Bessel van der Kolk

One of trauma's more notable features is its power to disconnect our minds from our bodies so that we can survive pain—both physically and emotionally. Think of how victims of sexual or physical abuse often describe being outside of their bodies during violent incidents. This disconnection is an involuntary tactic that numbs pain and allows them to survive the trauma. The process of reconnecting involves regulating the ANS so that we don't get stuck operating out of the wrong branch.

Let's start with an example. While driving down a familiar street in your neighborhood, you see a car run a red light, barreling toward the driver's side of your car. Without any conscious thought or effort, your muscles tighten to create full body tension (including your hands gripping the wheel) as you brace yourself for possible impact (trauma). The car swerves away at the last second, narrowly missing a powerful collision.

After having come to a screeching halt during that four-second experience, you "shake it off", lightly press the gas pedal, and ease your way back into the flow of traffic.But you're still gripping the wheel. Your jaw's still clinched, your breathing is still shallow, and your shoulders still painfully hunched towards your ears. Your body won't release this tense, contracted posture or breathing pattern until it feels safe again.

What happens if your mind keeps replaying the near-death experience, looping the terrifying near miss again and again, even as you make dinner or get ready for bed? There's no safety signal from your mind. In turn, your body will remain in a tightened, hyper vigilant state long after the physical threat.

This prolonged tightness marks the beginning of what many of us experience as chronic physical pain. Emotionally, you may find it difficult to remain calm the next few times you get behind the wheel—setting off a habit of anxiety and panic when you drive.

Processing emotional trauma

The body has been designed to renew itself through continuous self-correction. These same principles also apply to the healing of psyche, spirit, and soul.

—Peter A. Levine, *Waking the Tiger: Healing Trauma*

Warning: This is where many of us get hung up when moving past the trauma that underpins most cases of chronic anxiety and depression. We expect some complicated, scientifically complex, nearly impossible (or even expensive) set of steps. None of those are true.

Like the previous example about the lingering effects of the stressful traffic incident, much of what we experience currently is an automatic response that served a purpose during the initial event but caused more harm than good in the present. If we consider that the ANS changes the "automatic" bodily functions like heart rate and respiration, then it shouldn't come as a surprise that the most effective activities for regulating the nervous system include bringing those functions into a steady state. And thanks to a number of free, reputable resources online, access to the teachings are as close as our smartphones.

What ancient indigenous cultures have known for centuries about trauma has finally made its way to mainstream Western medical science. We release through our bodies and we heal in community.

Processing and releasing emotional trauma is shockingly simple—meaning there aren't a lot of complicated steps— but by no means easy. It takes attention, intuition, consistency, patience, support, and an openm mind. The same combination of natural and body-based (somatic) methods that worked—and continue to work—for me may not work for you. But if you're committed to healing, I encourage you to play the long game.

Experiment and pay close attention to the results—without judgment! During this phase of learning and healing, replace right vs wrong with calm vs upset. Notice what activities, environments, and people contribute to a more regulated nervous system and sense of well-being.

And for the love of all things holy: Let it be simple! Don't give into the inevitable thoughts and feelings of "this can't be all I have to do to rescue myself from hell". Although anticlimactic and even a bit counterintuitive at times, it most certainly is all you have to do. But here's the catch: you have to keep doing all the things that resonate over and over and over. We're using our bodies as the powerful vessels they are to intervene and   break the mental patterns that cause us to suffer. It's the gift that keeps on giving—if we practice.

Somatic techniques and practices for releasing trauma

When a young tree is injured it grows around that injury. As the tree continues to develop, the wound becomes relatively small in proportion to the size of the tree. Gnarly burls and misshapen limbs speak of injuries and obstacles encountered through time and overcome. The way a tree grows around its past contributes to its exquisite individuality, character, and beauty.

—Peter A. Levine, *Waking the Tiger: Healing Trauma*

Unhealed trauma is often at the root of chronic anxiety and depression, and consistency and awareness hold the keys to your healing kingdom. As you begin practicing somatic healing techniques, let the process be messy. Let grace work on your behalf. Don't beat yourself up or get discouraged when you lose your rhythm. Make a note, then get back to the practices.

Like when you learned to ride a bike, play an instrument, or shoot a basketball, the time will come when it just clicks.

Instead of spiraling into a full-blown panic attack when preparing for a big presentation or getting hit with an unexpected expense you don't have enough to cover, you stop. You create that golden space between stimulus and response. You reach for a somatic activity that takes you out of the spiral and back onto solid ground.

Below are three broad categories under which my somatic healing and self-regulation practices fall. Whether you gravitate towards several (like me) or just one or two, be open. Be patient. And above all, listen and be kind to yourself on this leg of the journey.

#1: Breathwork

Breathwork is a general description for breathing techniques that intentionally channel and focus on the breath. This practice tops my list because it's so easy to reach for. We can do it anytime, anywhere, no matter what—regardless of physical pain or limitations.

While the autonomic nervous system (ANS) also controls involuntary bodily functions like blood circulation and gastrointestinal activity, our breathing is the one automatic function we can quickly take off of autopilot and make a conscious activity. The other quality that makes breathwork an attractive somatic healing practice is that there's no pressure to clear your mind or do anything other than focus on your breath.

There are several well-known and research-backed breathwork techniques, and one of my go-to is box breathing. This four-step technique goes as follows:

- Take a deep breath in for four counts (place your hands below your rib cage to be sure that you're inhaling fully).

- Hold your breath for four counts.

- Exhale for four counts.

- Hold again for four counts.

It's magic for breaking through the worst feelings of anxiety or depression. I promise!

#2: Mindfulness and Meditation

While mindfulness and meditation aren't synonymous, I lumped them together here because—in my experience—one generally leads to or supports practicing the other. Both terms, having become more popular in the Western wellness arena, receive definitions that range from broad and esoteric to narrow and hyper-prescriptive. That's why (as usual,) I'd like to start by providing what I use as working definitions for each.

Mindfulness

When searching for a working definition of mindfulness, I landed on one set forth by Dr. Jon Kabat-Zinn—a professor and the founder of the world-renowned Mindfulness-Based Stress Reduction Clinic. He defines mindfulness as "the awareness that arises through paying attention, on purpose, in the present moment, non-judgmentally."

What I love about this definition is the inclusion of non-judgement, which allows us to bring a sense of neutrality and calm to the here and now.

As it relates to releasing trauma, anxiety, and depression, I use mindfulness much like I use breathwork. It's what I affectionately refer to as my mental "stop, drop, and roll" for when my negative thoughts and emotions converge to ignite an internal firestorm. More specifically, I find that engaging as many senses as possible makes the practice more effective and can make everyday moments feel like magic.

Meditation

The Cambridge Dictionary provides what I consider one of the more simple and straight-forward definitions for meditation: "The act of giving your attention to only one thing, either as a religious activity or as a way of becoming calm and relaxed." What I find most attractive about this definition is that it doesn't include the need to clear your mind because—as any novice or experienced meditator will tell you—clearing your mind is a herculean feat! This definition also steers clear of any prescriptive postures like sitting cross-legged on the floor or holding your hands in a particular position.

There are many benefits to bringing your attention to only one thing, but I love the way Deepak Chopra puts it:

"...meditation solves the problem of the divided mind by opening the door to a whole mind." And since trauma's primary mechanism is to disconnect and divide, the idea of using meditation to unify our minds (thoughts, emotions, and physical sensations) makes it a powerful tool for moving beyond chronic anxiety and depression.

My meditation journey started over 20 years ago when I began going to hot yoga sessions. However, I didn't truly integrate it into my mental health practice until 2013. I often joke that life brought me to my knees, so I decided to flip over onto my butt and give meditation a real try!

For me, the trick was to not take it so seriously. Instead of thinking about getting it right, I focused on exploring different styles of meditation, finding what resonated with me, and showing up consistently. Whether you meditate for three minutes or 30, sit on a meditation pillow or lie on your back in bed at the end of the day, keep coming back to the stillness. Let the practice take its course! Build the muscle of singular mental focus and watch it transform how you heal and move through your life.

#3: Movement

At first, trauma being "stored" in the body might seem like a bit of an overreach (at least it was for me.) But if we go back to the idea that trauma is what's left behind after a painful or stressful encounter, then it may seem more plausible.

Our bodies continue producing hormones and chemicals to fight, flee, or shut down, even though the original threat to our physical or mental safety no longer exists. Those chemicals have no real-time use or outlet. Over an extended period of time, this cycle creates disharmony in our musculature, as well as our immune, pulmonary (heart), and endocrine (hormonal) systems. The result: bodies that won't stop hurting (chronic pain) and other prolonged physical illnesses like heart disease and autoimmune conditions.

So how exactly do we use movement to remove trauma from our bodies? Below are practices and programs that can help reconnect your brain's sense of safety to the rest of your body's real-time experience, moving it out of the past danger and into a feeling of safety and balance.

Yoga (there are several kinds to explore)

Somatic Experiencing (Dr. Peter Levine)

Trauma Release Therapy (Dr. David Berceli)

EMDR (tapping)

Healing in Action: Radical Truth-Telling Meets Relentless Self-Compassion

CHAPTER IV

"I don't like myself."

These were the four words I cried into the phone while talking to my sister-in-law one January afternoon in 2015. I'd reached yet another rock bottom and needed to talk to someone I could trust with both my words and my heart.

I'd decided to move my son and I back to Baltimore after only being in Phoenix for five months.The landing back home had been quite bumpy (to put it mildly) both emotionally and financially. My decision to return stemmed from a vivid and powerful dream. In it, a distant yet familiar voice told me that I'd need help securing my son's emotional and social wellbeing as I finished this leg of my healing process.

While my ego was pretty mortified at the prospect of going back home for help, my instincts knew to comply. This wasn't the first time in my life that voice had come to me, and I couldn't deny its track record of divine timing or its complete accuracy.

A few years later when I reflected on this linchpin moment, it dawned on me that I probably heard the voice (I still shy away from labeling it God) because I'd weaned myself off of the anti-anxiety medication that I'd become far too reliant on. My mind and body could communicate without a toxic interpreter. The uninterrupted connection made trusting myself a far less risky endeavor.

I don't know how to explain what came after that phone call other than a profound yet contradictory mix of sadness and levity. It was almost like the scene in the *Wizard of Oz* where we find out that the all-powerful wizard is just a regular guy in a cheap, shiny suit behind a fancy curtain. There it was, laid bare for me to see and feel: I did not like myself—at all. Not one bit.

The way I looked, the way I felt, where I lived, how I interacted with my son, what I did for work (and the fact that I was still searching for work,) my continued engagement in harmful, pseudo-romantic relationships—nothing. None of it. It was all trash, and I'd finally said it to myself out loud. And, thanks to my sister-in-law, I had a witness.

If you've ever confided in or confessed a deep, dark secret to a loved one before, then you've experienced how the immediate barrage of guilt and sadness quickly give way to—or is at least joined by—a surprising sense of relief. It's the emotional /mental/physical "Yes, finally!" moment when you can breathe again—even if only for a few moments.

This fleeting moment of freedom between confession and repercussion: that's the feeling you'll need to hold in your heart and your mind's eye as you move into this next step of freeing yourself from anxiety and depression. It's what truth feels like. It's what happens when your body, mind, and spirit are in full agreement. You'll need to recognize that all-encompassing bliss as you introduce yourself to life outside of chronic anxiety and depression.

The purpose of suffering is to help us locate our internal divisions, reclaim our reality, and heal these inner rifts.

—Martha Beck, The Way of Integrity

You've begun addressing and clearing out the ghosts of traumas passed. You're aware of the intimate (and biological) connection between trauma, your body, and your emotions. You're learning how to interact with yourself as an unbiased and nonjudgmental observer. And instead of operating on autopilot, you've begun questioning everything you thought you knew about how your life is "supposed" to look and feel and be. Amazing! These are all foundational and necessary benchmarks in this framework.

But when it comes to escaping the grips of chronic anxiety and depression, phase four is what I've come to identify as the "now what?" phase. It's where we put our new knowledge and theories to the test.

Once you accept that a deep disconnection from yourself, along with unreleased pain and wounding (not an incurable brain chemical imbalance) are the root causes of your ever-present anxiety and depression, it's impossible to unsee it. You'll reach your internal crossroad, maybe even your own version of my "I don't like myself" revelation.

And if you're like me, this new discovery will catapult you into a season of voracious study. Psychology, spirituality, religion, science—you name it! It's all fair game as you peel back the layers of your self-loathing or grief or shame or unforgiveness, searching for the exact coordinates of your wounding and disconnection.

Then, after all of the books, podcasts, and YouTube videos, after the weekend retreats with experts and gurus, the vibrancy and exhilaration after each "aha" moment... nothing. You've connected the dots from the past to the present, the path from there to here, a thesis that answers "why am I like this?" emerges, satisfying the parts of you that needed psychological closure. Great... but now what? How does all this new-found information lead to the end of your suffering?

If you've reached this point—or when you do—don't get stuck! Your knowledge is not power if you don't apply it. This is where you decide (yes, *decide*) that you want to move from theory to application, from knowing to doing. It's at this fork in the road that you get to move from "why?" to "what's next?" Here, you choose your own adventure: operate within the same painful, predictable patterns or venture down a promising, yet uncharted path of freedom from your chorionic mental and emotional turmoil.

But remember healing, at its core, is simply the process of change with the goal of restoration and wholeness. And all meaningful internal change begins with earnest, sincere self-inquiry and the willingness to answer honestly—no matter how bad it hurts. From there, you'll begin trusting yourself again, building an experience of awareness, connection, and harmony that clears a path for the work in the next phase of this framework.

As Martha Beck puts it, "Getting out of hell doesn't mean picking up a new set of chains, a new set of absolute beliefs. It means replacing rigid convictions with curious openness, to your own sense of truth in every moment." For me, this phase is where I realized that nothing is worth the peace and freedom I gain when I commit to telling myself the truth and lovingly holding myself with kindness and self-compassion—whether that truth is painful, pleasant, or somewhere in between.

Self-Inquiry: Telling the Truth to Yourself about Yourself

Facts and truth really don't have much to do with each other.

—William Faulkner

Before jumping into this part, I think it's important to draw the distinction between fact and truth. This may seem like splitting hairs, but when it comes to cultivating deep self-awareness and internal honesty there's a critical distinction. Here's why: while facts can exist without a declaration of truth, truth exists as a combination of measurable facts, context, and a subjective (i.e., emotional) interpretation.

An exercise I'd use when explaining this key nuance to my English Composition 101 students involved a question of distance. First, I'd ask the class to write down how far away they lived from campus (it was a community college, so everyone commuted.) Then, I'd ask if that distance was near or far. I'd end by asking them to write down their mode of transportation.

The result: more often than not, even if students commuted nearly the same distance to campus (the measurable fact,) how they traveled (context) determined whether they considered that distance to be near or far. Students who walked or rode their bikes three or four miles to school were more likely to say they lived far from campus in comparison to those who drove. Is either group's conclusion that four miles is near or far from campus less truthful than the other? Not at all.

To make the distinction between fact and truth more personal, think about a time when you began a workout routine or learned to play a musical instrument. The same "heavy" 10-pound dumbbells that you struggled to complete eight bicep curls with during day one feel more like paper weights after two months of consistent training. In the case of learning how to play the piano, the same scales that you stumbled through—likely with frustration— after your first lesson become easy warm ups after a few weeks of practice. Did the weight of the dumbbells (the fact) change? No. Did the keys on the piano magically rearrange themselves to make it easier for you? No. Did your assessment of truth—whether the 10-pound dumbbell was heavy or not—change? Yes. The difference between the fact and the truth: your context and interpretation.

Truth=fact + context + (emotional) interpretation

Telling yourself the truth is an act of profound self-love and liberation. It's a practice that, once strengthened and refined, serves as the needle and thread for mending the internal divisions at the core of chronic anxiety and depression. The trick is to always remember that your truth will change over and over and over again, which means telling yourself the truth requires vigilance. You must pay attention to your whole self—what you feel, think, and do daily—as you shift and grow out of the patterns that have kept you stuck in pain.

In my experience, the process of identifying your truth requires the repetition of two key steps: 1) asking yourself empowering, self-reflective questions, and 2) actively identifying and interrogating the stories you tell yourself.

1: Self-inquiry and questions that lead to your truth

There are entire spiritual schools of thought surrounding the concept and practice of self-inquiring (absolutely fascinating if you're into that kind of thing!) But for our current purposes I think it best to keep it simple and literal: self-inquiring is the act of questioning yourself. This is where we start combining phases one and two of the Through You, To You framework with intention.

Asking quality questions about our internal workings and answering as the unbiased observer will make space for truth to emerge. Combining these two intentions is a superhighway to truth, a road not congested with the vehicles that transport emotions through the past, present, and future—all of our stories. This consistent practice of questioning and answering without judgement creates an emotional and psychological safe space to explore all possible answers.

Think about it: you're far more likely to share the truth of your most recent bout of depression with a friend you can trust to both comfort you and encourage you to get out of bed and take a shower. But if you don't feel safe enough to share, chances are your friend's "Hey, how've you been?" text will be met with a lackluster "I'm good, just busy" or a guilt-ridden response two days later, "Sorry I'm just responding."

So, exactly what questions work best for digging ourselves out of depression and anxiety? How can we use self-inquiry to increase self-awareness? Here's a rule of thumb I learned from one of my metaphysical and spiritual heroes, Dr. Michael Beckwith: ask empowering questions. Ask questions that move you up and forward, not down and back. This is critical because (if you remember from chapter one) our brains are wired to answer questions. We don't let them go. As such, the quality of your question directly impacts the quality of your answer and consequent thoughts and feelings.

To get you started, here are a few examples of how to change questions from *back and down* ones that perpetuate our current stories to *up and forward* inquiries that uncover facts that lead to something new.

Questions you might ask when you're feeling anxious or depressed

Down and back questions	Up and forward questions
What's wrong with me?	What activities have I engaged in that leave me feeling bad about myself?
Why can't I just snap out of it and get out of bed?	What are two small actions I can take right now to feel more energized? What would help me feel safe right now? How can I support myself the next time I start feeling this overwhelmed?
Why do I always wait until the last minute to [fill in the blank]?	What feelings am I avoiding when I decide not to [fill in the blank]? What do I need help with so

	that I can clear my calendar and some mental space to complete my task on time? Have I said yes to doing something that I really wanted to say no to?
Why do I keep letting [fill in the person's name] run all over me?	What do I think will happen if I begin setting boundaries? What am I afraid of losing by standing up for myself? How can I respond the next time [fill in the person's name] disregards my needs? How can I show myself forgiveness?

Questions to increase self-awareness

When were the last three times I felt excited about a project (personally or professionally)?

What would a perfect day look like during the workweek, start to finish?

How do I react when someone misunderstands something I said or wrote? Did I lash out at the person? What was my internal dialouge about myself?

When did I have my last three panic attacks? What was happening inside of me and around me right before it started?

What are five characteristics I believe a good mother/star employee/excellent mate *should* possess?

How do I talk to myself when I make a mistake?

In my everyday life, am I usually motivated by fear or excitement?

2: Identifying and interrogating your stories

If you watched the Emmy-nominated family drama, *This Is Us*, you may remember Randall and Beth's couple's game, worst case scenario. It's a no-holds-bar, no censorship, no judgment session where the married couple go back and forth letting their anxiety and worry spiral completely out of control. Children, career, family, marriage—anything. Most catastrophic scenario wins.

I simultaneously laughed and wept the first time I saw one of my favorite tv couples play this game because I felt so seen. I wasn't the only one doing this! I'd never seen anyone else go through this terrifying yet freeing exercise of exposing and integrating the chaotic flurry of scenarios in their minds. In fact, it's how I'd summon the courage to come outside of my self-imposed box and take action when faced with doubt and worry of the unknown.

By actually answering the often rhetorical question, "What's the worst that could happen?" my inner control freak could get ahead of any possible problems or make some semblance of peace with whatever possible shipwreck my imagination conjured.

Those worst case scenarios they shared with each other (or wrote down in my case) about how the family would be left destitute and homeless if one of them switched careers, started a business, or how their children would become jail-bound and drug addicted if they didn't attend the best elementary or middle school, are examples of stories we tell ourselves. But what's so genius about this exercise is that it drags our mental boogeymen from under our bed of silent rumination. And once we pull them from the dark recesses into the light of day, they do one of two things: expand or shrink. In my experience, it's almost always the latter.

While this game illustrates the obvious stories we tell ourselves, the most impactful ones are the insidious stories that play on repeat in our heads—unconsciously and unchecked. Many of today's neuroscientists, mental health professionals, and personal development experts liken our unconscious stories to computer programs. They're an amalgam of beliefs, values, and experiences installed on the hardware of our minds—when we're young and malleable— and run just about every facet of our lives—including when and how we experience chronic anxiety and depression. It may sound like an exaggeration, but I promise, it's not.

Fear, to a great extent, is born of a story we tell ourselves and so I chose to tell myself a different story.

—Cheryl Strayed

Finding and interrogating the stories you tell yourself—especially the ones that cause fear and helplessness and self-loathing—is an advanced version of the self-inquiry process. It's the kind of questioning that leads to radical truth telling. It requires playing detective inside of your own life, examining the various pieces of evidence you've amassed (your feelings and experiences) to reverse engineer and uncover the culprit. More often than not, you'll discover that your faulty beliefs and stories (the inputs) are the bandits, constantly stealing your peace and stifling all of your well-intended efforts to heal and grow.

My approach to this more advanced self-inquiry: keep it simple. I decided that my inner detective should be an eight-year-old, much like the example I gave earlier in the book. But instead of allowing the wounded and frustrated adult me to stop this imaginary kid's questioning with a huffy "because I said so," I found my stories by pausing, reflecting, feeling the discomfort, and telling myself the truth in spite of how terrible or ridiculous it sounded.

Let me be clear: if you decide to go with it, this kid's barrage of whys and how comes will make you squirm! On top of that, having to throw up your hands and answer "I don't know" more times than you'd like during the innocent, unrelenting questioning may leave you depleted, angry, or both. Don't let the eight-year-old beat you!

It's perfectly ok not to have all of the answers. In fact, you'll probably shrug your shoulders and throw up your hands more times than not as you begin to investigate. I can't begin to recount all of the times I asked myself questions like "Why did you blow this month's budget by going out for that extravagant Wednesday night dinner?" or "Why did you wait until you had 48 hours left before starting a project you had two weeks to complete?" only to be met with crickets—or the occasional bout of tears if I really lost my cool.

But what did we learn about a meaningful question? It's the mental equivalent of that sock that slips off your heel in your sneaker while you're on a walk. It won't let you rest until you either fix it or decide it doesn't matter. So, even though you may shrug it off in the moment (or let the inner eight-year-old drive you to tears,) the question of why you acted against your own self-interest will remain. It may take two or 20 more self -sabotaging episodes for you to identify what you've been telling yourself at the moment. When I began letting my inner eight-year-old question my stories at the height of my chronic depression, it usually went something like this:

I'm on day two of laying in bed with the blinds open, sun shining in, half-listening to one of my favorite HGTV series drone on in the background, only getting from under my blanket to use the bathroom or grab the takeout I'd asked the delivery driver to leave at the front door.

For the life of me, I have no idea why it feels impossible to move. I'm not sick. I've been in bed sleeping on and off for almost 48 hours, so no lack of rest. What's stopping me from getting out of bed and engaging in my life?

My answer: I'm just so tired!

Inner eight-year-old: Why are you tired after so much sleep?

My answer: I don't know! There's so much running through my head. All of that thinking feels overwhelming and exhausting. It's all too much!

Inner eight-year-old: What's "it" and what thoughts are running through your head?

My answer: LIFE is too much! Ugh! I don't know, just... thoughts! Like all of the work I have to do for my job, folding the laundry overunning the basket at the foot of my bed, wondering why I can't seem to get any words on the page for that article my client already paid for, mad at myself for not paying attention when I was supposed to be watching tv with my son the other day, worrying about money, worrying about money some more... ALL OF THE THOUGHTS!

Inner eight-year-old: Why are you thinking all of the thoughts?

My answer: They never stop. Ever. There are always soooooo maaaaany thoughts! It makes me tired.

Inner eight-year-old: If they never stop, that means they're going even when you're not in bed, right?

My answer: I mean, I guess...

Inner eight-year-old: So what's the difference between all the thoughts running through your head when you're in bed and when you're out of bed?

My answer: Ugh! I don't know! I guess the difference is that, when I'm not feeling overwhelmed and tired, I'm only focused on a couple of the thoughts. I act like the rest of them aren't there. I don't switch back and forth between them as much.

Inner eight-year-old: Great! Sounds like a plan to me. See you in the shower!

During my darkness and depression, unbiased self-inquiry helped me find the story that rendered me utterly useless and forlorn in bed for two days straight: life is too much.

All of my thoughts and emotions are too much and they overwhelm me to the point that I have no energy for life's most basic tasks. If this sounds like something a dramatic teenager or even a toddler throwing a tantrum would say, you're correct!

Much of the trashy, untrue, unconscious stories we tell ourselves stem from the unhealed childlike parts of us who never learned to regulate their nervous systems, emotions, and thoughts. You're stuck in trauma's time warp, disconnected from the truth of your present-day life, your divine ability to feel and think differently here and now. Those negative thoughts and feelings produce chemicals within the body that reinforce the fatigue, and lethargy—it's a cycle. That's likely the *real* reason you haven't made yourself get out of bed.

If you're anything like me, you're thinking "Are you kidding me? That's it?" The answer is yes, that's exactly it. Because your inner eight-year-old isn't emotionally invested in the faulty story you've told yourself—that you can't get out of bed because it's all too much—they can ask all of the innocent questions you won't. More importantly, they don't need to craft some complicated solution. As an unbiased participant in your internal process, they're able to point you in the direction of what you already know: you're making it hard on yourself by not focusing on thoughts and feelings that bring you energy and life.

This is where we run into the main culprit: beliefs. If you keep finding and interrogating your stories, you'll collide with the core beliefs that have allowed these stories to live rent-free in your head for decades at a time. In my life, I've found that all of the unhealthy stories I told myself that lead to years of suffering and self-loathing were based on two foundational beliefs: I am not enough (or I am not worthy,) and that anything good must come through struggle and pain. Dismantling those beliefs and replacing them with my new truths—I am worthy of all things good, and I can experience good things with ease and grace—was and continues to be my simple, effective guard against chronic anxiety and depression.

Ideas to Consider: Your Body Is Your Personal Lie Detector

Not sure if you're *really* telling yourself the truth about what you think or how you feel? That's ok–your body knows! Just like polygraph tests (aka lie detectors) measure changes in breathing, heart rate, blood pressure, and perspiration, you can train yourself to ask questions, then listen to your body for a confirmation of truth (or deception.)

In an article written for *Psychology Today*, the author summarizes that:

"The polygraph rests on the principle that psychological states reliably lead to physiological changes in the body. More precisely, when people are lying,... they often experience fear, shame, anxiety, guilt, and worry... Those emotional states then trigger physiological changes in the body that can be detected with the polygraph. The physiological changes are driven by the sympathetic nervous system in a process that is often referred to as the fight or flight' response."

Essentially, lying to yourself is a response to a thought, emotion, or action you subconsciously perceive as dangerous or harmful. Often, when this happens, it's because there's a misalignment or disconnection between what you're thinking, acting, and feeling. Telling yourself the truth is the first step in bringing them into alignment.

Here are three steps for using your innate lie detecting abilities on yourself:

1: Ask a question while you're still

It doesn't matter if you're sitting or standing, at home or outside. Just be sure to ask yourself a question while your body is still. The question should be as simple as possible to avoid bringing too much mental activity into the answer.

2: Answer the question out loud or on a piece of paper

Speaking or writing your answer automatically introduce your body into the process. You don't get a chance to sensor it as quickly as you would if you answer in your head. You'll notice if your voice changes pitch, volume, or speed or if your hand shakes you write.

3: Notice how your body reactions—without judgement

Pay attention to if your jaw clenches or releases, whether your shoulders raise or lower, if you fold in on yourself or if you sit up taller and open up your chest. Take note if you suddenly have butterflies or queeziness in your stomach, or if it settles down from previous uncomfortable activity.

Even if your answer isn't pleasant or agreeable, you'll feel deeper, slower breathing, a steady heart rate, less stomach discomfort, and an overall sense of calm when you're telling the truth.

Self-Compassion: your passport into the world of inner freedom

Where we think we need more self-discipline, we usually need more self-love.

—Tara Mohr

As you can guess, asking yourself empowering questions and answering them honestly isn't always sunshine and rainbows. Even after uncovering these troublesome stories and beliefs, you'll likely be left with feelings of guilt and shame. You may also begin to wonder "have I really believed that foolishness all of my life?" Yup, you sure have!

While you continue to heal yourself from chronic anxiety and depression, it's crucial to generate and live from a deep well of love for yourself and for others. You'll need to connect what has been disconnected through trauma and to replace the lies that wound with the truth of your divine humanity. If that sounds like a tall order, I'm happy to report that there's a linchpin practice that—once you turn it into a habit—makes loving yourself as automatic as brushing your teeth in the morning. The secret to your undying love for self and others: self-compassion.

Self-compassion is the prerequisite for your self-love. That's because it removes all conditions that you've unconsciously placed on loving every part of you—past, present, and future. Coming face-to-face with the truths you've uncovered, the faulty beliefs that you didn't even know you had, may leave you feeling cold, sad, and shaken. But when you begin basking in the warmth of self-compassion, you discover the transformative power of "anyway."

The Power of Relentless Self-Compassion

Learning how to offer myself self-compassion changed everything. As I stumbled through my process of asking empowering questions, answering as an unbiased witness, uncovering my negative stories, and telling myself the truth, life got messy—internally and externally. The problem with that is I'm a neat freak. I don't do messes.

This whole process of telling myself the truth, of knowing better—and actually working to do better—threw me head-first into yet another trauma response: my perfectionism. I was fighting decades of unconscious programs like shutting down instead of opening up, procrastinating instead of pausing to breathe. Remaining vigilant so I could catch myself before slipping into destructive patterns proved to be one big, exhausting mess! Working to change my patterns and apply my healing practices reminded me of a toddler learning to use utensils to feed herself. Most of the food missed her mouth, landing on her fat cheeks and bib, or out of frustration, she'd revert to using her hands instead of the spoon.

During that period, still listening to and reading everything I could get my hands on about deepening my connection to spirit and myself, I ran across a quote from another one of my all-time favorite spiritual teachers, Dr. Wayne Dyer. In his book *The Power of Intention*, he writes, "Be good to yourself. You are a manifestation of God, and that's reason enough to treat yourself kindly."

While the idea that simply being alive makes everyone worthy of kindness and love may seem like a no-brainer, it was completely foreign when I thought about it concerning myself. You mean I don't have to be good enough or smart enough or hard-working enough for someone (including myself) to offer me kindness when I'm having a hard time?

You mean that when I disappoint myself, I'm not being too lenient if I just let it go? You mean telling myself "It's okay, you're still getting used to new responses and emotions and thoughts" doesn't mean I'm making excuses or not holding myself accountable? Correct. In each of those scenarios, showing myself kindness was simply acknowledging those stumbles and missteps as part of my humanity.

After reading Dr. Dyer's take on worthiness and self-compassion, I decided— from that day forward—to show myself compassion anyway. No matter what. My new "anyway" practice meant that no matter how imperfectly I stumbled through applying the techniques, tricks, tools, and practices for change, I resolved to give myself a mental and emotional soft place to land, to wrap myself in self-compassion anyway.

Almost like magic, after a short period of living by my "anyway" practice, the relentless self-compassion I grounded myself in was the very force that flung open my heart's doors. I actually began loving myself as the kind, beautiful piece of the Infinite that we're all made of. It also helped me see that same light in others, even when they were acting otherwise.

When you begin shining the divine light of relentless self-compassion towards yourself, it'll catapult you further along your path of healing from chronic anxiety and depression than the mean-girl (or guy) approach you've likely taken thus far. You'll begin living in the knowledge that the journey from knowing better to doing better and ultimately feeling better exists in parallel with—not in opposition to—your ability to make peace with each misstep, over and over and over again.

To get you moving on your path of loving yourself to connection and wholeness, I'd like to start by providing a working definition of self-compassion (if you haven't noticed by now, working definitions are a thing for me!) So what exactly is self-compassion?

About three years after beginning my "anyway" practice, one of my closest friends introduced me to the work of Dr. Kristen Neff, researcher and co-founder of the Center for Mindful Self-Compassion. In her 2003 paper, *"The Development and Validation of a Scale to Measure Self-Compassion,"* Neff lays out the components of self-compassion, and how to measure it in a clinical setting as a tool for helping individuals live with less anxiety, depression and improve their overall mental health and happiness. She points out that the word compassion literally means "to suffer with," reminding us that compassion inherently acknowledges the pain one is feeling in the moment—not what we *should* feel or think. More specifically, Neff explains:

"Compassion involves being open to and moved by the suffering of others, so that one desires to ease their suffering. It also involves offering others patience, kindness and nonjudgmental understanding, recognizing that all humans are imperfect and make mistakes. Similarly, self-compassion involves being open to and moved by one's own suffering, experiencing feelings of caring and kindness toward oneself, taking an understanding, nonjudgmental attitude toward one's inadequacies and failures, and recognizing that one's own experience is part of the common human experience."

The Three Elements of Self-Compassion

1. Self-kindness vs. Self-judgment.	2. Common humanity vs. Isolation.	3. Mindfulness vs. Over-identification.

(Neff, 2003)

Also, because it's a powerful component of emotional intelligence and self-awareness, people with high levels of self-compassion tend to demonstrate higher levels of resilience, integrity and operate from a growth mindset.

What self-compassion is not

Another critical step that Neff takes when defining self-compassion is pointing out what self-compassion is not. Why is this distinction important? Because in our Western culture, where we routinely celebrate people who keep a "stiff upper lip" and tough through difficult situations, being kind to yourself in the moments you may not feel you deserve it can induce even more guilt and self-hate than the actual events that are causing you pain and suffering.

That's why Neff strategically points out that having compassion is not synonymous with self-pity, self-indulgence, or self-esteem. In other words, don't confuse or conflate giving yourself grace with feeling sorry for yourself, letting yourself off the hook, or artificially boosting your self-image in the moment.

I'd like to add two more ideas to her list, ones that came in handy as I worked to replace the mean girl that inevitably showed up (and sometimes still raises her voice) during my times of emotional suffering. Self-compassion is not passive, nor is it toxic positivity. It's an active practice that moves and creates positive momentum as you move towards wholeness and internal connection.

Self-compassion doesn't require you to ignore the facts when you're facing terrible situations or feel anxious or hopeless. Instead, offering yourself self-compassion allows you to acknowledge your suffering—self-inflicted or not—with the understanding that nothing you do or think or feel or experience can make you less worthy of your own love and kindness.

Applying self-compassion as part of your healing journey

Having compassion starts and ends with having compassion for all those unwanted parts of ourselves.

—Pema Chodron

One of the many things I love about Neff's three parts of self-compassion is that it gives you options. There are times when it's easier for me to access one of the three components than the other, allowing me to gain some traction in the process so that I don't spiral into anxiety or depression.

I found success in my "anyway" practice, which aligns with what Neff identified as the kindness over judgment component of self-compassion. However, during the times I've had to battle my perfectionist tendencies (which, consequently, fueled bouts of anxiety and procrastination,) I found that reminding myself of our common humanity served as the best approach. By reminding myself perfect humans don't exist, I found energy to show myself the self-compassion needed to navigate through the emotional storms.

On your path to the new you, even after you've acknowledged the impacts of trauma and set yourself free from chronic anxiety and depression through mindful, deliberate, imperfect practice, you'll continuously uncover parts of you that make you cringe. These parts may make you want to shrink and hide into your shadow self. Don't forget that self-compassion is a warm, bright light—use it!

You may choose to be mindful in a moment of depression by noticing your thoughts and emotions without identifying them as a part of you. You may decide to offer yourself kind, loving words after realizing you've fallen back into a pattern of emotional eating. You may even remind yourself that everyone makes mistakes when you give a less than perfect presentation at work or snap at a loved one in frustration.

Remember: whichever component of self-compassion grounds you in self-love is the best one to reach for. Be relentless and fearless in your application of self-compassion. Never give in to the temptation to shame or guilt yourself back into the version of you that demands perfection, that doesn't allow the inevitable missteps along your path. By doing so, you'll build the habit of showing up for yourself with the kindness and love and support you'd give to anyone else in your life who you love. No matter what, you deserve it.

Stage 3
EXPRESS

Who Would You Be If You Weren't You?

CHAPTER V

He allowed himself to be swayed by his conviction that human beings are not born once and for all on the day their mothers give birth to them, but that life obliges them over and over again to give birth to themselves.

—Gabriel García Márquez, Love in the Time of Cholera

A few years ago, while on Youtube, I stumbled upon world-renowned author, researcher and lecturer Dr. Joe Dispenza talking about one of his best-selling books, *Breaking the Habit of Being Yourself*. The video stopped me in my tracks. I'd never considered that my "self"—the person I identify as, the self that had experienced so much mental and emotional pain and suffering over the past 40-plus years—was really just one big, intricate habit. How was that even possible?

As I began considering the validity of Dr. Dispenza's claim, it made me think of a common social norm we've all experienced in the U.S. Whether at a dinner party with strangers, a job interview, or a first date, the familiar request that someone inevitably makes within the first couple of minutes of engagement is, "So, tell me about yourself."

We usually answer that question after quickly and unconsciously considering what parts of ourselves would resonate and be best received in that context. You might lead with your job title or your marital status. You might mention being a parent, a college graduate, a cancer survivor, where you grew up or your favorite weekend hobbies. But are those roles and activities and achievements and experiences really *you*?

The answer: yes and no.

Who Are You, Really?

Much of what we consider to be our self hinges on the socially-constructed version. It's a compilation of the things we have, do, or have done, roles we fill and how we relate to people and the world around us. However, roles and interests often begin and end. We stop doing certain activities and replace them with new ones. Painful situations recede, becoming less a part of our current narrative and more of our histories. We move from being Director of Finance to retiree, from mother of two young children to an empty nester who's rediscovering her love of dance or learning to play the guitar.

To make it personal, here's an exercise that quickly reveals the fragility and ever-changing nature of what we call "the self."

Ask yourself, who am I? Write down the first few things that come to mind.

Next, ask yourself if you were *you* before the list of descriptors and roles you likely just wrote down. Hint: the answer is yes.

Repeat that pair of questions for another round or two and you'll either get frustrated, confused, or—if you're like me the first time I took myself through the line of questioning—you'll conclude that the only real you that hasn't changed is... a mystery. You likely won't quite know what to call it.

"It" is the living energy inside that's been there since before you were born. "It" has witnessed you build, remodel, and tear down each version of your socially-constructed self. It's the "you" that came into the world with your body and will leave this plane when you do. As that exercise points out, our true selves are a part of the great unfathomable, a piece of the greatest unknown. I call it God.

And the best part: that makes us all the same: pieces of God walking around in human form. Pretty mind-blowing and heart-opening if you truly let that sink in! Even if you don't believe in God, you may at least settle on the idea that it's impossible to describe your true self in terms of anything fixed or measurable.

But since most of us humans don't walk around introducing or describing ourselves as little pieces of God or the great unknown, let's stick to the versions of self that we're in charge of! Here's a straightforward definition of what I'm referring to as the socially-constructed self: it's our sense of who we are as individuals. It includes our identity, personality, emotions, beliefs, goals, and experiences that make us unique.

The self develops over time through our interactions with others and the world around us. It's influenced by our biology, upbringing, culture, and personal choices. A strong sense of self allows us to maintain an integrated identity, understand our own needs and motivations, and establish meaningful relationships. Though the self feels coherent, it's also complex, with different aspects that may seem contradictory.

In essence, the self is the individual, subjective experience of our own existence as a person. It's the inner world of thoughts, feelings, perceptions, and memories that we carry with us throughout life.

Getting to know ourselves better helps us discover the qualities inherent within the unchanging self. From there, we're better equipped to create and integrate our changing self with our Godlike-self—this version of self being constant before external influences like trauma, anxiety, and depression.

Redefining Yourself Outside of Anxiety and Depression

Some of you may miss the person you were never free to be. If you grew up with constant trauma and stress, you may never have been able to be at home with your self... Once you acknowledge being disconnected from yourself, you begin to recognize all the ways you have been distracted from this longing for home.

—Thema Bryant, PhD, Homecoming

Creating the next version of yourself may seem daunting or difficult or downright impossible. You may've never considered that you could live a life without constant fear and anxiety, or that you could generate enough love and gratitude and peace that you felt energized to consistently engage in life without forcing yourself.

Maybe you're not even completely convinced that you're the designer and creator, the architect, engineer, and master builder of who you are and how you show up in the world. That's ok. Wrapping your mind around such a massive honor and responsibility can intimidate even the most convinced convert—like me.

As I write this book and share my Through You To You framework, I'm in the midst of what I consider my first fully-conscious creation cycle. I'm petrified!

In fact, the process of writing this book, along with the idea of putting it out to help others, unearthed a level of self-doubt and fear of rejection that I didn't know still existed within me. I found remnants of feeling behind in life, of begrudging the time "wasted" mired in the muck of mental quicksand.

Also, I found myself falling into an old pattern that doesn't serve me. I'm notorious for trying to jump from intellectual understanding to positive action without that middle step of acknowledging and honoring the feelings that accompany deep change. This all-important step on the path to internal connection and integrity—that middle passage between knowing better and doing better—is what neuroscientist and cultural anthropologist Mario Martinez calls "mourning the known misery." Not only do we mourn the misery, we may still engage with it as we cling to parts of ourselves that have been our default settings.

Thankfully, the previous stages in this framework—questioning everything, viewing those answers as an unbiased and non-judgmental witness, confronting the deep internal disconnection caused by trauma, telling ourselves the truth and interrogating our stories, all while showing ourselves relentless self-compassion as we put our healing practices into action—have prepared us for this beautiful, empowering, and magical stage. Those practices allow us to create our own programs and establish new default settings that align with the version of ourselves we want to express.

I revisit parts of the framework almost daily, using the practices to show up for myself as a compassionate friend or to snap myself out of a faulty story about what's possible for my life. As you go through the process of redefining what it feels like to be you, remember: your personal version of this framework will always be available to reorient yourself in this process of evolution and creation.

At some point, scared though you are, you'll no longer want to look back. You'll feel the pull to go forward—not as the same person doing different things, but as a different person. —*Martha Beck, The Way of Integrity*

As I mentioned, this is where I am on my path—finished mourning, but lacking a clear, crisp vision of my new version. Not the most comfortable position, but it beats the alternatives I've experienced!

Removing chronic anxiety and depression from your identity isn't an overnight process, but it doesn't have to be riddled with pain either. As you begin thinking about what this phase might entail for you, here are three invaluable ideas that've kept me sane and inspired. By centering these foundational principles in my mind, I'm able to infuse curiosity, creativity, and joy as I navigate life's terrain toward full expression.

Three key considerations for redefining yourself

#1: You are a human being, not a human doing

I started here because it's so easy to get stuck in the paradigm of defining yourself by familial roles, professional occupations, or the activities you engage in during your free time. But I encourage you to try this on instead: What qualities do you want to embody and express? How do you want to show up for yourself and for others in your life?

When I asked myself this question, my immediate answer: I want to show up as loving kindness. I want to show up as a peacemaker and a problem solver and a safe space. Your list may be wildly different than mine, but redefining yourself by who you "be" instead of what you do grants you access to a whole host of possibilities. It also connects you to the qualities most intrinsic to your unchanging self.

And eventually, the titles, roles, and stories that limit how you engage with life become less important. You can be whatever qualities you choose no matter your career, your marital status, or whether you follow a raw vegan diet and rock climb for fun. Who you are becomes less of a performative exercise and more of a deliberate daily practice.

#2: You are present tense

I began my career as a digital marketer in 1999, just as internet advertising—and the internet itself for that matter—started making its way into the mainstream. One of the trends I distinctly remember from that time was advertising campaigns that promoted a company as "reimagining how we [fill in the blank with an everyday task]."

From banking to buying books to communicating with friends who'd moved across the country, the internet fundamentally shifted what it meant to operate in our society at large.

Not unlike the dawning of the internet age (and now the dawning of the mainstream commercialized use of artificial intelligence,) creating the version of you who's unburdened by chronic anxiety and depression requires you to reimagine what it means to be you—in the present.

Your past should not define your current reality. You get to divorce yourself from old habits that defined you. The present-day you can begin forming the habit of creating space after a familiar stimulus, enacting a more ideal response that aligns with who you want to experience yourself as.

Just like we still shop and deposit checks and communicate with loved ones who live far away—but in vastly different ways post the internet revolution—so it will be in your life.

It continues to shock and amaze me that I can experience an almost identical day-to-day life in a completely different way today.

The same work project or personal finance problem that would've set off a panic attack or a bout of severe procrastination and denial now triggers a series of questions about what's really happening on the inside and a hefty dose of self-compassion for the fact that those feelings exist... because I'm human.

Lastly, your friends and family are human too. So while you're giddy and excited to live as a new and improved version of yourself, it may not go over so well with them. It's not because they're malicious and don't want to see you happy. Your changes inherently disrupt aspects of your relationships. Hear me clearly: they have every right to opt out!

Just as you have the right to explore and stumble through and try on new versions of you, they get to decide that the changing you doesn't work for them. You may even find interactions with your closest friends and family getting tense, awkward, or less frequent as they constantly remind you of who you've always been. Again, it's ok.

Don't be tempted to build a negative story around what's happening, creating victims and villains in your head. Let these natural shifts and relationship shake-ups come and go, but don't let anyone—including you—try to hold you to the past and patterns that don't align with who you're creating in present tense.

#3: Experimentation is your friend

We can learn and change in a state of pain and suffering, or we can evolve in a state of joy and inspiration. Most embrace the former. To go with the latter, we just have to make up our minds that change will probably entail a bit of discomfort, some inconvenience, a break from a predictable routine, and a period of not knowing.

—Dr. Joe Dispenza, Breaking the Habit of Being Yourself

This last consideration has been the gift that keeps on giving! Letting myself off the hook, not expecting myself to have all the answers fully formed in my mind, has set me free from the tyranny of needing to get it right the first time—or the fifteenth time.

I've applied my love of science to this process of redefining myself outside of anxiety and depression. Viewing this phase through the lens of the scientific method provides both structure and perspective for using all of the tools and practices in an almost endless array of combinations until I find what works.

Founded in the mid-1500s, the scientific method is a process scientists formalized to study and understand the world around them during a time where theories about the natural world hinged primarily on a mishmash of anecdotal evidence and religious and spiritual teachings.

As many of us learned in middle school science class, the six steps in the process are something like this:

1) Make an observation.

2) Ask a question.

3) Form a hypothesis or testable explanation.

4) Make a prediction based on the hypothesis.

5) Test the prediction.

6) Iterate: reflect on the results, draw a conclusion and use them to guide next steps.

What I love about applying the scientific method to our internal environment is that trying on new beliefs and behaviors based on the previous outcomes—what scientists call iteration—allows for repetition and refinement based on fact, not story. The goal of the method, whether applied to the world around you or inside of you, is to arrive at principles and laws that provide consistent, verified explanations and solutions.

One important note about successfully using the scientific method: it's most reliable when you test one thing at a time. Scientists call this controlling the variables. It's easier said than done in our real lives, where an uncountable number of occurrences exist outside of our control. But when your experiment can get close to testing only one variable, it's easier to determine a clear cause and effect relationship. That means you have a better chance of knowing if your new belief or behavior moves you towards your desired expression. Here's a quick example:

Observations:

—I currently wake up at 7:30am and feel anxious and rushed in the morning.

—Research shows morning routines can help improve energy and reduce stress levels.

Question: How can I wake up earlier and feel less stressed in the morning?

Hypothesis: If I adjust my sleep schedule to wake up 30 minutes earlier and add a morning routine, then I will feel more in control of my mornings.

Test:

—For 1 week, wake up at 7am and engage in a morning routine — make bed, meditate, exercise, shower, and eat breakfast.

—Record if I feel less anxious in the morning and throughout the day.

Results:

—Waking up earlier and performing a routine helped me feel less anxious in the mornings.

—My energy stayed higher until the afternoon.

Conclusion: Waking up 30 minutes earlier and going through a morning routine decreases my anxiety and improves my energy in the first half of the day.

While this example technically introduces two variables (waking up early and adding a morning routine,) you get the point. Breaking the habit of operating as the anxious, depressed version of you will require intention, self-awareness, and patience—not having all the answers or flawless implementing your healing practices. Trust the process and your intuition.

Take the Limits off of Your Next Version

Imagination is more important than knowledge. Knowledge is limited. Imagination encircles the world.

—Albert Einstein

Who you've been and where you are now on your healing journey pales in comparison to the endless possibilities for how you get to show up for yourself and in the world. You get to choose—we get to choose — without limitations! One of the most humbling aspects of our human experience lies in our capability to actually conjure up a thing from the recesses of our being and bring it into reality. Such is the case with the next version of you.

Equal parts magic and mess, fully connecting your mind, body, and spirit will require a continuous flow of imagination to wash away your current limited self-concept. Imagining what's possible is the starting point for revealing a version of yourself that doesn't struggle under the weight of trauma-induced anxiety and depression. There's a version of you who knows that growth and grace operate simultaneously, wrapping your whole, integrated self in its bespoke garment of inner safety, abiding peace, and deep gratitude.

At the end of *The Way of Integrity*, Martha Beck writes about "imagination as salvation." Noting that our human capacity to conjure and hold an imagine in our minds, then bring it into existence has gifted us everything from alphabet to the iPhone, she writes:

"The way we see determines what we see, whether our primal world shows us a universe that's dangerous, frightening, and meaningless, or safe, enticing, and alive."

Here's my wish for as you walk the path through you, to you: instead of using your imagination to replay the past or project negative possibilities of the future, treat it like a piano or a paintbrush, as an instrument and a tool for creating art and beauty.

You're both the maestro and the music, the painter and the color palette. You are inherently capable and worthy of the next and best version of yourself. If you're reading this, it's your time.